**The Center
for the Advancement of
Teaching and Learning**

SELECTED PAPERS
from the
15th INTERNATIONAL CONFERENCE
on
*COLLEGE TEACHING
AND LEARNING*

**Edited by
Jack A. Chambers**

*Florida Community College
at Jacksonville*

ISBN 1-931997-02-0

Center for the Advancement of Teaching and Learning, *Florida Community College at Jacksonville*, 501 W. State Street, Room 441, Jacksonville, FL 32202.

CONTENTS

FOREWORD

The Center for the Advancement of Teaching and Learning (CATL) was developed in 1987 when Florida Community College at Jacksonville accepted K. Patricia Cross' challenge to use the classroom as a modern laboratory for conducting experiments to gauge the impact of teaching on student learning.

The philosophy of the Center for the Advancement of Teaching and Learning is that classroom teachers are the key to improving student learning; the Center is therefore composed of faculty members under the guidance of a steering committee which consists of faculty from each of the four major campuses of the College. Part of the Center's success can be attributed to the numerous opportunities given to faculty to test their teaching ideas and to put research results into practice.

Center Steering Committee members serve as Campus Mentors and as sponsors of faculty development programs, both college-wide and on each campus. The Center also supports faculty mini-grants for classroom research and professional development and sponsors a number of awards honoring teaching faculty. The Center itself has been the recipient of an award—the Theodore M. Hesburgh Certificate of Excellence—for its faculty development programs.

In an effort to stimulate creative discussion and promote experimentation to improve the teaching/learning process, as well as to honor those who have already significantly improved learning in higher education, the Center annually sponsors an international conference. The conference features recognized educational leaders in diverse areas of teaching, learning and technology. Since its inception the conference has grown steadily and now attracts nearly 1,000 scholars annually from around the world. This publication, *Selected Papers*, was created as a result of Center interest in honoring faculty who develop some of the most outstanding contributions to the conference. It also preserves and makes available the contributions made to the teaching profession as a whole. *Selected Papers* is abstracted in ERIC and covered online by the American Psychological Association's PsycINFO.

Many people are responsible for the success of the annual conference. We would like to thank all participants, including featured speakers and workshop leaders; presenters from universities, liberal arts and community colleges throughout the United States and abroad; faithful attendees; and Florida Community College faculty and staff who give so generously of their time and efforts each year to help the conference continue its success.

Both the international conference and the *Selected Papers* journal have increased in growth and focus over the years. This year's publication contains articles selected as the 15 best papers of those submitted to the *Fifteenth International Conference on College Teaching and Learning;* they represent a cross-section of nearly 300 faculty presentations. All papers submitted for consideration in this year's journal were reviewed by the Florida Community College faculty members listed below. Papers were judged on the following criteria:

- Quality of content

- Quality of writing and presentation

- Focus of the paper
  (i.e., teaching, learning, technology)

- Discipline

- Appeal to an audience of professional, post-secondary educators

- Theoretical or practical applications

We hope you will find the ideas presented here applicable and inspirational to your own teaching, learning and research. Please plan to join us at the *Sixteenth International Conference on College Teaching and Learning*, March 29-April 2, 2005, in Jacksonville, Florida.

Victoria McGlone
Librarian

Stephanie H. Powers
Professor of Communications

John Mullins
Professor of Biology

Courtney S. Summerlin
Professor of Legal Studies

Ronald S. Wolf
Professor of Culinary Arts

MONARCH GENERAL HOSPITAL:

VIRTUAL PRACTICE SETTING

FOR NOVICE NURSING STUDENTS

Phyllis D. Barham
Old Dominion University

INTRODUCTION

The United States faces a severe nursing shortage. Currently licensed Registered Nurses (RNs) practicing in this country are aging, and over the last decade fewer students have entered nursing education programs. The Division of Nursing, within the Bureau of Health Professions, predicts that demand for full-time equivalent RNs will begin to exceed supply by 2010 (American Association of Colleges of Nursing, 2002a). The U.S. Bureau of Labor Statistics projects the need for more than one million new and replacement nurses by the same date (American Association of Colleges of Nursing, 2002b).

The challenge for schools of nursing is to recruit and educate persons prepared to pass the national licensure examination for registered nurses (NCLEX-RN) and enter a demanding workforce. In this workforce, higher patient acuity levels and persistent shortages of professional nurses increase demands for complex psychomotor skills combined with astute clinical reasoning and critical thinking skills.

NURSING EDUCATION

The practice of nursing combines the art of caring with the knowledge of the sciences to provide holistic support to a client/patient (hereafter patient). Nurses consider the bio-psycho-social aspects of each patient when developing a nursing diagnosis and plan of care implemented independently or in conjunction with a physician's medical regimen. "Nursing knowledge and technical skills are no longer adequate to meet the complex healthcare needs of the population; critical thinking and clinical reasoning are essential." (Dearman et al., 2001, p. 169).

Critical thinking is well described in nursing literature and while no one definition is universal, recurrent expressions used to describe the skill involve logic, reasoning and clinical decision-making. (Di Vito-Thomas, 2000; Martin, 2002) Helping nursing students to attain the scientific knowledge, master psychomotor skills, and then apply them in a logical organized manner while communicating their interest in and concern for the patient is a true test of multi-tasking and a challenge to nurse educators.

Some students may be quite adept at regurgitating memorized facts; still others excel in communication techniques or hands-on skills. Assisting students in applying their knowledge in a variety of situations and under diverse circumstances while maintaining the safety of the patient and the integrity of the plan of care can be a daunting task—especially with beginning nursing students. Preventing students from becoming disillusioned as they compare nursing, as often portrayed in the media, with the actual practice, is important as well. When unrealistic ideas of nursing practice conflict with the reality of actual practice, a student may abandon the field and choose another career.

Nursing education typically requires the acquisition of a knowledge base prior to the commencement of clinical practice. Lectures and skills laboratories comprise the basis for learning theory and the psychomotor skills specific to nursing.

Students not familiar with the acute care practice setting often have difficulty envisioning how they will put their newfound knowledge and skills to work upon entering the educational phase of "clinical practice." They express anxiety about their abilities to interact with the patient, the family, the staff, to know what to do, how to do it, when to proceed and most of all, they worry about harming the patient with their inexperience.

The literature illustrates how nurse educators have creatively tried to meet the need for simulated learning in a safe environment using critical thinking vignettes (Chau et al., 2001; Van Eerden, 2001), case studies (Baumberger-Henry, 2003), and role playing (Gray, 2003). In addition to these methods, a safe place to allow students to begin to apply knowledge and skills yet retain a semblance of an acute care setting led this author to the development of a virtual hospital.

MONARCH GENERAL HOSPITAL

The full-service acute care virtual facility was implemented in 1999 with beginning nursing students. Instructional and technical support was provided by the university's Center for Learning Technology. Using a hospital/medical facility metaphor, the Website offers a Web-based entrance to "visitors" as well as "employees" via the Internet.

The "visitor" entrance to the Website is not restricted and anyone who knows the URL can open these pages. The "visitor" can then view student-generated information about Monarch General Hospital in the following categories:

- General Information

- Missions And Goals

- Services Offered

- Affiliations

- Board Of Directors

- Administrative Staff

- Hospital Directory

The "employee" entrance is access restricted to Old Dominion University nursing students, faculty and selected staff. Students "enter" the employee zone of the hospital by providing a secure username and password which grants access to special project areas as well as the hospital directory where nursing students are able to:

- View patient chart information

- Receive oral and written reports from staff nurses, clerks and physicians

- Receive new orders

- Interact with a variety of virtual patients

In addition, students are able to take advantage of the library and media content available in the Monarch

General Hospital media center. To further extend the hospital/medical facility metaphor, a set of floor plans was implemented to give students a visual concept when considering the logistics of moving about the facility in addition to the text-based directory.

Special Project Areas

A representative special project area is Nursing Leadership and Management where students complete budget, staffing and scheduling, and organizational chart projects. Student receive guidelines for the projects online and submit their final projects for display on the Website as a supplement to their in-class and group activities. Other special project areas include Phone-a-Nurse, Research News and Daily Quotes, and Change Affirmations. All of the special project areas utilize text and graphics in HTML.

Patient Charts

Each unit has a "rack" of patient charts from which students select an individual case that is the target of a particular assignment. Depending upon the type of exercise, some cases are more elaborate and interactive using multimedia than others.

Oral and Written Reports

To simulate receiving reports from other personnel—nurses, clerks, physicians, etc—both audio and text versions of the information are made available to all students. This not only simulates a real-world type of experience where some of the communication is oral and some is written, it provides flexibility for any technical limitations students may have while navigating the site. For example, a campus-based computer lab may not allow playing audio files under normal circumstances, so students are able to view the alternate text format and continue an assignment. The audio clips are currently delivered using RealMedia® video streaming technology to accommodate low bandwidth (56k modem) environments and standards-based delivery (RealPlayer™ and RealOne™). Text objects are delivered in HTML. The provision of both text and audio also increases accessibility to people with disabilities.

Interaction with Patients

Interaction occurs on two levels. The first level may be described as "observation and response" where the student views chart-based information, hears and/or reads reports from other staff, and then views video clips of patient behavior. The information gathered in those formats is then used to complete a variety of assignments such as creating a nursing care plan to be submitted to the class for discussion and review. The video clips are currently delivered using RealMedia® video streaming technology.

The second level of interaction with patients may be described as "query and feedback" where the student poses a typed question in a Web-based application to a virtual patient that then provides the student with feedback based on pre-determined key words. The student continues to ask questions and the virtual patient continues to provide feedback until the student has gathered enough information to build a health history. The dialogue is tracked in the Web-based application in chronological order and can be saved and/or printed to share with other students for discussion and review in class or online in threaded discussion.

Macromedia's Director was selected to prepare this Web-based application based on the breadth of multimedia file types that can be integrated and by the ease content can be optimally deployed across multiple platforms. The player is one of the most widely distributed playback technologies on the Web. A stand-alone version (CD-ROM) is also available that provides text-to-speech technology so that the virtual patient replies audibly as well as in text. Text-to-speech is available in the Web-based application to those students whose systems provide voices at the system level.

Library and Media Center

A variety of Web-based narrated graphic presentations, full motion video presentations, as well as electronic reserve articles are available to the students to simulate the availability of resources in a hospital environment. Faculty, other students, third-party vendors, etc. may provide these multimedia presentations. Electronic resources extend to library services available through the university library.

Monarch General Hospital has been integrated into beginning level courses in the Bachelor of Science in Nursing program in a variety of ways and provides a means for measuring and reinforcing content and skills mastery prior to initial clinical experiences.

The Ambulatory Clinic

Students are oriented to the Monarch General Hospital during fall semester in an initial nursing course, Health Assessment. This course teaches students the skills required in attaining a complete health history and performing a thorough physical exam. Content is presented over the 14-week semester organized by body systems, and students in the laboratory setting work in pairs examining each other and recording results.

Therapeutic communication skills and accurate recording of data (both history and physical findings) as well as examination techniques are emphasized. Prior to the use of Monarch General Hospital, health history information as a lab report was graded by faculty solely on the basis of the content presented in the report. Accuracy of the data, or thoroughness of the health history data collection were not possible since faculty did not/could not sit in on the interviews between lab partners. Using patients in the Monarch General Hospital ambulatory clinic allows students repetitive practice in health history taking skill and allows faculty to measure accuracy as well as report format.

"Patients" of all ages and backgrounds were developed for the Ambulatory Clinic. Each patient presents a "chief complaint" related to one of the body systems matching the course format. A photograph of the patient along with the statement of the chief complaint appears on student's computer screen.

As queries taught for gathering specific data related to a patient's chief complaint are predictable, a lexicon including key words in the set of questions to be asked was developed. Upon seeing the patient and the statement of chief complaint, the student types questions to be asked of the patient. The patient's response is triggered by the key word(s) in the question and a text-based response appears on the screen for the student to note.

Upon finishing the interview, students then access the Monarch General Hospital patient chart and develop the written "history of chief complaint" to be submitted for faculty review. The repetition of interviewing patients throughout the semester allows students to become adept at history taking, and allows faculty to determine student accuracy, provide feedback and corrections.

The General Surgical Unit

During the second semester of the BSN curriculum, students focus on fundamental skills of nursing. The first half of the semester students practice the skills in the school's skills laboratory, once again using each other or manikins as simulated patients. Students learn the content and practice skills in a disconnected format (patient hygiene or bed making one week, sterile dressing change or intra-muscular injections another week) and are expected to integrate both theoretical content and psychomotor skills in the practice setting (clinical experience) during the second half of the semester. It is just preceding the clinical practice portion of the semester that student anxiety levels are highest. They worry that they will not know or will not be able to remember what to do when responsible for their patient in the clinical setting.

Mr. Calamity. To help in allaying anxiety and to help students begin to critically think about the variances they will encounter with individual patients, the General Surgical Unit client, "Mr. Calamity" was developed. Mr. Calamity is a virtual older patient (reflective of the average age of hospitalized patients in the United States) admitted to Monarch General Hospital following an auto accident and emergency surgery. Students are introduced to Mr. Calamity during the first week of the semester and complete a critical thinking exercise each of the five subsequent weeks prior to attending lab each week.

Mr. Calamity's needs simulate the content/skills being taught each week. Students receive a verbal report from the "night nurse," can see the patient chart including the physician's orders and a photograph of Mr. Calamity reflective of his present condition.

Students work in small groups using a Blackboard discussion format to formulate a plan of care for Mr. Calamity. Each week on a rotating basis, a student in each group must take a leadership position, facilitate the discussion and compile their group's consensus for the plan of care. Each group leader provides the faculty with a written report and verbally presents (and defends) the plan to the remaining groups in the lab.

Lively discussion ensues as the students are actively engaged in the process and practice critical thinking skills in the plan formulation. Students benefit from their five-week experience with Mr. Calamity as they are required to recognize important data and cues for Mr. Calamity or the staff or environment, prioritize the nursing actions needed and strategize how to proceed with the plan of care. After five weeks of assimilating data and planning care for Mr. Calamity, students are better prepared for their initial clinical experiences where they must put into action the plans developed.

Patient Education

Throughout Monarch General Hospital there are patients who need instruction about their conditions or how to care for themselves upon discharge. Patient education is a pervasive thread in nursing and students must learn the essentials of the teaching/learning process for application with diverse patients. During the fundamentals of nursing course, students are able to practice patient education with virtual Monarch General Hospital patients assigned each week. A photograph of the patient needing instruction is provided and student groups collaborate on identification of the learning need(s), development of objectives, learning outcomes and an evaluation measure.

Student group leadership is rotated with the leader charged to facilitate the discussion on Blackboard and provide both a written and oral report for in-class presentation. This exercise helps students begin to identify the numerous opportunities for patient teaching, recognize variations in teaching and learning styles, and realize that the patient education is not complete until evaluation shows content mastery.

Critical Thinking Exercise

While all of the patients in Monarch General Hospital inspire student critical thinking to some degree, a culminating sophomore level group exercise encourages students to work collaboratively in planning the care for several patients simultaneously. In the real world of hospital nursing, RNs are often responsible for the care of many patients while supervising the care provided by ancillary personnel. Students assigned only one or two patients while in school find the real world of nursing to be quite shocking as graduates, and some are unable to cope with the complexity of caring for multiple patients in a high stress environment.

The culminating sophomore critical thinking exercise allows students to visit the General Surgical unit and to see and hear the verbal report of the night nurse. Video clips are used to help the student visualize each of six patients described. The unit secretary (or ward clerk) gives a video presentation of general information and the nursing assistant chimes in with her morning report as well. Students are then able to "make rounds" on the six patients with video clips depicting each patient and patient room as it appears at the end of the morning report.

Recognizing cues from the night nurse, unit secretary, nursing assistant and patient charts, prioritizing needed actions and strategizing how best to meet each patient's needs are the objectives of the exercise. In addition, students must decide if and what actions might be delegated to ancillary personnel. Students clinical groups work together to develop a plan of action; lively discussion inevitably ensues as the groups then report to the entire class and debate their decisions.

SUMMARY AND CONCLUSIONS

Nursing education requires creative, interactive strategies to engage students in not only acquiring knowledge, but in mastering the critical thinking and application of psycho motor skills with diverse populations in a variety of health care settings. "Increased patient acuity, and the ambiguity of various patient care situations, requires complex decision-making as nurses attempt to sort extraneous from relevant cues in practicing the art of nursing " (Baumberger-Henry, p. 191).

Providing a safe practice site (no one has died because of student malpractice in Monarch General Hospital) for beginning students to initiate their nursing critical thinking skills within controlled patient situations was the goal of this project. Helping students to virtually explore the nurse–patient relationship and professional responsibilities prior to actual clinical experience helps inexperienced students develop a more realistic view of health care practice.

Registered nurses comprise a large portion of the current health care delivery system and the current shortage and projected shortages of registered nurses poses a threat in this country. Well-educated registered nurses are crucial to the provision of high quality health care services in the United States both now and in the future.

REFERENCES

American Association of Colleges of Nursing (2002a). *Nursing education's agenda for the 21st century.* Retrieved November, 2003 from http://www.nche.edu/ Publications/positions/nrsgedag.htm.

American Association of Colleges of Nursing (2002b). *Nursing shortage fact sheet.* Retrieved November, 2003 from http://www.aacn.nche.edu/Media/Backgrounders/shortagefact.htm.

Baumberger-Henry, M. (2003). Practicing the art of nursing through student-designed continuing case study and cooperative learning. *Nurse Educator, 28*(4), 191-195.

Chau, J., Chang, A., Lee I., Lee, D., & Wootton, Y. (2001). Effects of using videotaped vignettes on enhancing students' critical thinking ability in a baccalaureate nursing programme. *Journal of Advanced Nursing, 36*(1), 112-119.

Dearman, C., Lazenby, R., Faulk, D., & Coker, R. (2001). Simulated clinical scenarios: Faculty–student collaboration. *Nurse Educator, 26*(4), 167.

Di Vito-Thomas, P. (2000). Identifying critical thinking behaviors in clinical judgments. *Journal for Nurses in Staff Development, 16*(4), 174-180.

Gray, M. (2003). Beyond content: Generating critical thinking in the classroom. *Nurse Educator, 28*(3), 136-140.

Martin, C. (2002). The theory of critical thinking of nursing. *Nursing Education Perspectives, 23*(5), 243-247.

Van Eerden, K. (2001). Using critical thinking vignettes to evaluate student learning. *Nursing & Health Care Perspectives, 22*(5), 231-234.

Note: The author wishes to acknowledge the invaluable assistance of June Ritchie, Instructional Designer in the Center for Learning Technologies at Old Dominion University.

UNNERVING THE PEACEFULNESS

OF ONLINE LEARNING

Gerald D. Baumgardner
Pennsylvania College of Technology

INTRODUCTION

Like many transactions and activities conducted over the Internet, faculty have attempted to make online learning efficient and effective. Unfortunately, over the past few years, various individuals and entities have created (some with malicious intent) problems to hinder this efficiency and effectiveness. These problems merit attention and must be resolved in order to continue to improve online learning.

Although the Internet is designed to promote communication it also serves as a tool for disrupting such communication. These disruptions come in many formats and occur for various reasons. Del Russo (2003) notes that attacks on school networks are increasing exponentially and are coming from various individuals including students, faculty, staff, alumni and many unaffiliated individuals. Education-based computer networks are susceptible to crime as both insiders and outsiders tend to find easy access into these widely open systems.

Since all sectors of society are using the Internet as a way to buy or sell goods and services, higher education is no exception. Technology's importance continues to grow on campuses just as it has in the public and private sectors (Forte, 2003). According to the National Center for Education Statistics, 99% of all schools have access to the Internet (Charp, 2003). Additionally, faculty and students involved in online learning are vulnerable to the problems inherent in Internet activity. Universities want to provide open access to students, faculty, and staff. However, this open exposure makes it almost impossible to stop Internet-based attacks (Danford, 2003).

As more individuals are involved in Web-based courses, they become targets to various disturbances. These disruptions take many forms but can be broadly categorized as spam, viruses, hacking and spyware. Such problems impact the flow of effective online learning and have long-reaching effects on the online participants. For example, spammers are obtaining e-mail addresses at will (including those with .edu affiliations) and using them on a continuous basis throughout the Internet. David Heckman of Microsoft Research states that spam could soon represent 90% of all e-mail (Schwartz, 2003a).

EVALUATING THE PROBLEMS

In order to evaluate the problems posed by the above four Internet disruptions (spam, viruses, hacking and spyware) it's of value to look at some of the statistics which depict how each relates to online learning. These factors were researched and analyzed in order to arrive at some conclusions as to how to handle the problems.

Spam

To understand the magnitude of spam, one must imagine the number of e-mail messages passing through the Internet. It is not unusual for top spamming companies to send over 20 million e-mail ads per day (Baker, 2003). Half of all external corporate e-mail (or more than 2 trillion messages) will be spam, according to market research firm IDC (Swartz, 2003a).

Spam is a worldwide problem. Charp (2003) notes that 49% of Internet users spend at least 40 minutes a week deleting spam. This amounts to over 13 billion unwanted e-mail messages per day with an annual loss of over $10 billion in worker productivity in the United States alone, according to Ferris Research (Schwartz, 2003a).

Additionally, a study by the Pew Internet and American Life Project (2003) claims that 86% of Internet users find spam annoying or a big problem. Such problems have far reaching effects as they slow university-based computer systems as well as create problems for faculty and students whose e-mail addresses are available throughout the Internet. A self-analysis of an @edu email account used for an online-based course showed that spam activity increased by 80% over a one-year period. Such abuse is hard to stop as spammers have been using First Amendment protection to shield their activities (Woellert, 2003).

Online Learning. In relation to online learning, spam poses many potential problems, including:

- Spam sent from marketers to faculty and student accounts—this clogs much needed drive space while reducing faculty and student productivity

- Spam coming as a result of disgruntled students who share faculty and students' e-mail addresses in order to create or promote spam

- Spam that reduces the e-mail capacity of students connected to local Internet Service Providers (ISPs); although local connectivity is used, in part, to access online courses, spam has reduced the capacity of such accounts

- Spammers who have created methods for spamming bulletin boards and chat rooms, a critical communication component of online education. Although bulletin boards and chat rooms can be effective communication tools, spam could lessen the effectiveness of such devices.

Viruses

Faculty members are reporting high virus rates when downloading attachments. Such results indicate that viruses permeate many attachments and are likely to carry to the end user. Danford (2003) points out that such a problem is multiplied based on the number of infected machines along with the size and structure of the institution's computer system. During 2002 the cost for such viruses came to over $2.2 billion spent on anti-viral software (Hagerty, 2003). This has forced colleges to include anti-viral software in IT budgets. It is estimated that 5.4% of IT budgets will be spent on security with over 79% of all institutions including anti-viral software (Charp, 2003).

With .edu domains being one of the most commonly registered Internet domain categories, it is obvious that hacking poses a threat to colleges and universities. Even the non-edu servers that are registered as .com but support .edu structures could be as likely to be violated by hacking. This would include, for example, Web sites that support online education (such as publishers) as well as companies that supply platforms for offering online learning (such as WebCT and BlackBoard).

Forte (2003) mentions that the campus riots of the 70s have been replaced by, among other things, fears of crimes to campus computer systems. According to the FBI, system attacks are expected to reach 350,000 this year (Del Russo, 2003). Such breaches of security are sure to impact college systems. For example, the University of Texas reported that someone hacked into its campus computer system and stole the names and social security numbers of 52,000 individuals (Cain, 2003). Internally, students are using university systems to hack into other networks. This is leading to, among other concerns, identity theft. Information Week mentioned that such theft has impacted over 7 million individuals (Charp, 2003).

Online Learning. An informal study conducted at Penn College showed that, by the end of a semester of an online course, all class participants reported receiving some type of virus from class activity. This is a reoccurring problem as viruses continue to impact Internet-based education. The threat of viruses are limiting, slowing or crashing systems as well as reducing or eliminating valuable data (Fryer, 2003). Overall, viruses can impact online learning by:

- Spreading to class and college Web sites—this results in destroying information and reducing the speed of computer systems

- Infiltrating bulletin boards and chat rooms, disrupting or rendering inoperable these forms of online communication

- Mutating to the home-based personal computers of professors and students; this is extremely troublesome as individuals' computers tend to have fewer defense mechanisms than that of the larger institutional systems

- Creating a general state of chaos to the computer systems used for online education. Some online educators refuse to open attached files for fear of viruses. This forces students to submit work in alternative modes (including the traditional paper-based methods).

Hacking

Hacking into collegiate systems is fairly simple given higher education's penchant for free access to information and the need for academic freedom (Cain, 2003). Such systems are regularly "sniffed" for holes because most hackers know that such networks are not well secured (Del Russo, 2003). With such a large number of systems users and an interest in informational openness, it is easy to see how security is such an issue for colleges and universities. Additionally, hacking into online courses is a simple task as online courses are often given low status in terms of security (the general logic being that no one would want to hack into an online course).

Online Learning. Hacking could have far-reaching effects on online learning such as:

- Rendering a server ineffective which eliminates student access to online classes

- Destroying Web sites and files, forcing faculty to retrace and recreate class assignments

- Cutting the important links to libraries and other critical services provided to students—these links are vital in providing service for online students who rely on Internet activity for college services

- Attacking and destroying college sites, class systems, bulletin boards, chat rooms, calendars, grade databases, and other essential elements of online learning; although most information can be recreated, inconvenience is an issue

- Hijacking computer systems and either assuming student and faculty identities or stealing information for various reasons (recall that college systems contain a plethora of data that attackers could sell for profit, especially social security numbers, records and other components of personal data).

Spyware

Spyware applies to a range of programs that come bundled with screen savers, music-swapping software, and other downloads resulting in annoying pop-up ads— cookies which monitor the activities of the computer users and cookies used to take over remote systems (Hagerty, 2003). Such spyware allows individuals to track the activities of Internet users in order to, among other things, assume the identities of such users.

In 2003, A Drexel University student hacked into a TD Waterhouse account to make $46,000 in option trades. This was accomplished by using software called "The Beast" which monitors computer users by logging their keystrokes (Iwata & Swartz, 2003). Already, anti-spyware software sales are estimated at 10 to 15 million dollars annually (Hagerty, 2003). Such spending is needed to reduce the threat of spyware

Online Learning. Spyware creates problems for online learning by:

- Reducing productivity due to system slowdowns— these slowdowns occur because of excessive spyware that is attached to networks, thus reducing the speed and memory of such systems

- Creating annoyances that frustrate faculty and students—such annoyances could be pop-up ads, Web sites from which individuals can't exit, links that close browsers, etc.

- Monitoring the Internet activities of users—this becomes a form of online stalking that allows individuals to monitor activities of other users, possibly resulting in identity theft

- Storing data of computer users via cookies which are intrusive and act to slow the speed of Internet activity.

Overall

Overall, a critical look at any college-based computer system would result in the appearance of spam, viruses, and spyware along with the potential for attacks by hackers. Although spam and viruses tend to create the most problems, hacking and spyware are being elevated as considerable menaces to the world of online learning. All are part of a large trend in creating chaos for Internet users, including those involved in online education.

CONCLUSIONS AND RECOMMENDATIONS

Although online learning started as a simple yet efficient means of offering a variety of courses and topics to students via the Internet, it has experienced the same problems common to the entire Internet structure. Spam, viruses, hacking and spyware threaten to disrupt the true benefits offered by Internet-based education. While most problems started on the commercial sites, they have spread to include edu-based sites. One could hypothesize that online education has become, in many cases, commercial enterprise to the extent where success has created part of the problem. Wildstrom (2003) notes that we're no longer sure whether the PC on the desktop is a useful tool or a dangerous intruder to our privacy.

As with the commercial structure of the Internet, the answer to online learning lies in utilizing the network of entities with a vested interest in Internet-based education as the primary source for reducing such problems. Specifically, online educators and students, administrators, IT and Distance Education departments, software developers, internet and computer firms, and companies which support online education must share the responsibility of working together to reduce such problems.

In addition, governments must come forth to help in the fight against such problems. Utilizing laws and the court system could go far in dealing with these problems. It should be noted that the U.S. Congress has been working on such legislation (Swartz, 2003b). Also, several states have attempted to address such issues.

Recommendations for dealing with these problematic factors are multi-faceted. First, companies must continue to offer products that are more resistant to spam, viruses, hacking and spyware. This requires a strategy of remaining one step ahead of such groups in order to continue to create efficiencies for Internet education. For example, "Challenge and Response" is new software that could open the gates for a new generation of anti-spam technology (Ten Technologies to Watch in 2004, 2003). Second, colleges must continue to utilize anti-spam and anti-viral software, firewalls, and other products that minimize such problems. Third, Internet users (faculty and students) must use extreme caution in protecting passwords and e-mail addresses as well as utilizing caution in downloading files sent via the Internet.

In addition to the above, the Internet society must exercise caution in sharing and downloading information along with using appropriate software in order to reduce the threats caused by hackers, spammers, and virus or spyware spreaders. New laws should be enacted to aid in reducing the flow of unsolicited information and property destroying viruses (similar to the recent Do-Not-Call legislation). Such laws should be more rigid in penalizing violators. Databases should be protected in order to reduce the risk of hijacking personal information. A recently proposed law may help in this issue (Foster, 2003). Finally, an Internet user bill of rights or manifest may aid in reducing such problems (Wildstrom, 2003).

The combination of such activities should not be seen as a panacea but rather a set of actions that are necessary to reduce the online abuses involved with online learning. Ultimately, measures to prevent or eliminate such problems should help restore the original peacefulness felt within the online community. As with the classroom, environmental management is a key component of successful online learning.

REFERENCES

Baker, S., (2003, October 16). A stab at stemming Spam. *Business Week*, 115.

Cain, M., (2003). Cybertheft, network security, and the library without walls. *Journal of Academic Leadership, 29* (4), 245-248.

Charp, S., (2003). Security and privacy of information. *T.H.E. Journal, 9*, 8.

Danford, T., (2003). Blocking cyber attacks, increase bandwidth. *Syllabus, 11*, 35.

Del Russo, R., (2003). Securing your computer network. *T.H.E. Journal, 9*, 25-27.

Forte, S. P., (2003). A pragmatic approach to high-tech security on Campus. *T.H.E. Journal, 9*, 20-22.

Foster, A. L., (2003, October 17). Colleges' database dilemma. *Chronicle of Higher Education*, A35-36.

Fryer, W. A., (2003). A Beginner's guide to school security. *Technology & Learning, 9*, 9-14.

Hagerty, J. R., (2003, September 25). Unlikely German leads the war on Spyware. *Wall Street Journal*, B1.

Iwata, E., & Swartz, J. (2003, October 10). Student arrested in hacking, ID theft case. *USA Today*, B1.

Pew Internet and American Life Project. (2003, October 27). Spam bugs email users, survey finds. *The Patriot News*, B1.

Schwartz, E. I. (2003a, July/August). Spam wars. *Technology Review*, 33-39.

Swartz, J. (2003b, October 23). Senate passes anti-spam bill but many obstacles remain. *USA Today*, B1.

Ten technologies to watch in 2004. (2003, November). *Business 2.0*, 116.

Wildstrom, S. H. (2003, October 6). It's time for a new high-tech Manifesto. *BusinessWeek*, 32.

Woellert, L., (2003, November 10). Will the rights to pester hold up? *BusinessWeek*, 73-4.

PEER COACHING:

AN INVESTIGATION WITH STUDENT TEACHERS

Irene J. Caswell
Lander University

INTRODUCTION

The literature on student teaching/supervision in Colleges of Education has emphasized the importance for faculty to find ways to assist students who are preparing to teach to make connections between university coursework and teaching in the classroom (Garmon, 1993; Gormley, 1991). Factors such as the large number of student teachers assigned university supervisors, dispersed field locations and scheduling constraints tend to compromise effective supervision (Englert & Sugai, 1983). University supervisors typically have teaching and other responsibilities on campus in addition to supervising field experiences, which limit the amount of time they can spend in the field supervising, observing, and providing feedback (Anderson, Caswell, & Hayes, 1994). Peer coaching has been indicated as an effective means for assisting teachers to apply new skills and strategies, develop a sense of collegiality and professionalism and assume a reflective stance toward their teaching (Joyce & Showers, 1980; 1981; 1988; Showers, 1985; Showers & Joyce, 1996).

DESCRIPTION OF THE STUDY

Based on the value of peer coaching with in-service teachers reported extensively in the literature, four major questions were investigated:

1. *Would student teachers, like in-service teachers, see the value of peer coaching and what benefit, if any, would they perceive?*

2. *What difficulties or concerns would student teachers perceive as they engage in peer coaching?*

3. *Would these perceived difficulties change over time?*

4. *In what ways, if any, would student teachers perceive that peer coaching encouraged reflection?*

An integration of these areas of inquiry into a peer coaching model provided a means to investigate peer coaching as a tool for supplementing supervisors' feedback.

The four pairs of student teachers (N = 8), two males and six females, ranging in age from 22 to 23 years, were placed at three schools and volunteered to serve as participants in this study. Participants attended a three-hour peer coaching training session and four scheduled one-hour peer coaching seminars. The time table for the study is provided in Table 1.

Table 1
Time Table for Study

Week	Data Analysis	Activity
1	Collect participants' responses on initial interviews. Enter baseline data.	Initial training session. Initial individual taped interviews.
4 – 6	Transcribe tapes and collect peer coaching forms. Copy any journal entries. Begin member and theory checking.	One peer coaching cycle completed. 1st peer coaching seminar.
7	Transcribe tapes and collect peer coaching forms. Copy related journal entries. Look for patterns that might identify themes for coding to research questions. Highlight related terms. Continue checking.	Peer coaching seminar 2.
8	Transcribe seminar tapes and highlight for related terms. Continue data analysis.	Peer coaching seminar 3.
10 – 12	Transcribe seminar tapes and Exit interviews. Continue data analysis.	2 peer coaching cycles. Seminar 4. Exit surveys, interviews.

Peer coaching process information and a Framework for Peer Coaching Sessions (to guide scheduling and calendars) and Peer Coaching Data Collection forms were distributed. The general procedures were as follows:

Preconference. Student teacher and peer coach meet. Teacher shares lesson plan and selects focus for coach to observe and sets time. Coach clarifies purpose for observation and both discuss how to collect information.

Observation. Peer coach observes student lesson.

Postconference. Student teacher and peer coach meet within 24 hours of lesson observation. The teacher is asked to discuss the lesson. The coach shares feedback and data using non-directive conferencing style. S/he allows teacher to share first and then provides feedback of four types:

1. S/he comments positively on what the teacher did well during the observation period and notes why it appeared to be effective.

2. S/he clarifies the comments as needed to gain understanding.

3. S/he prompts teacher to explore alternatives.

4. S/he provides leading questions, suggestions, or recommendations to further enhance learning in the situation.

Qualitative data were collected to form the basis of the descriptive data using the following formats: 1) participants' audio-taped interviews and seminars; and 2) participants' provided written responses in Peer Coaching Data Collection forms and exit surveys.

FINDINGS

In regard to the first research question— *Would student teachers, like in-service teachers, see the value of peer coaching and what benefit, if any, would they perceive?*—results indicated student teachers perceived that peer coaching provided numerous benefits in five major ways. These included: 1) the ability to observe the peer coach's techniques; 2) the positive and helpful feedback provided regarding their own observed work; 3) other non-evaluative feedback; 4) the resulting reflection and ideas which they applied to their teaching; and 5) the opportunity for shared student teaching experiences.

Findings which addressed research questions two and three—*What difficulties or concerns would student teachers perceive as they engage in peer coaching?* and *Would these perceived difficulties change over time?*—indicated four areas of concern: 1) scheduling time; 2) giving and receiving feedback; 3) feeling nervous about being observed; and 4) making mistakes. Overall data on findings for these three research questions are provided in Table 2.

Table 2
Peer Coaching Combination Time-Order and Effects Matrix of Concerns and Benefits

	Initial Interview		Final Interview	
	Peer Coach Goals	Peer Coach Concerns	Peer Coach Benefits	Peer Coach Concerns
Participant A	Good learning experiences	Making mistakes	Self-evaluation of skills	None
Participant B	Peer feedback	Nervous about being observed	Peer feedback	Students being distracted
Participant C	Peer feedback	None	Planning & reflection on teaching skills	None
Participant D	Peer feedback	Time to observe	Peer feedback	Time
Participant E	Good learning experiences	Nervous about being observed	Observing techniques	Time
Participant F	Good learning experiences	Giving feedback	Peer feedback Observing techniques	Time
Participant G	Good learning experiences	Time to observe	Peer feedback Reflection	Time
Participant H	Good learning experiences	Getting peer feedback	Observing techniques	Giving useful feedback

Data to address the final research question—*In what ways, if any, would student teachers perceive that peer coaching encouraged reflection?*—were collected from audio-taped responses during peer coaching seminars and individual exit interviews. Participants were prompted to share their perceptions about peer coaching and reflection during four peer coaching seminars. They identified three areas that peer coaching had encouraged reflection: 1) teaching performance; 2) techniques; and 3) lesson ideas.   Responses on individual audio-taped exit interviews provided final qualitative data that peer coaching had encouraged reflection in the areas of planning, teaching, and analysis of teaching skills before, during, and following the lesson (Table 3).

Table 3
Peer Coaching Effects Matrix – Reflection (Exit Interviews)

Participant A	Peer coaching makes you plan to reflect; you have to think about when you're done and it helps you while you're teaching.
Participant B	Peer coaching allowed the two of us to sit back and reflect on each other's lesson and bring things up so we could start talking about it.
Participant C	Peer coaching encourages reflection by making you think after you're done with your lesson, not just waiting to hear what your peer has to say.
Participant D	When I went to observe, I saw the things that my peer was doing and I was impressed. I went back and said well I want to try that and be able to do that.
Participant E	Peer coaching really makes you reflect on the whole lesson. I got to where I could almost go play-by-play; I could just rewind it in my mind.
Participant F	My peer was able to reflect on the way I taught and I was able to reflect on the way my peer taught.
Participant G	Peer coaching encourages reflection because I looked at my peer's feedback and I thought about it and then I could reflect on my peer's opinion if I agreed or disagreed with it and think how I could change things.
Participant H	Peer coaching encourages reflection because it brings your attention to things you didn't notice before.

CONCLUSIONS AND RECOMMENDATIONS

Findings from this study, although based on a small number of participants, indicated support for the use of peer coaching with student teachers as a means to supplement as well as enhance feedback from supervisors. Five areas of benefit provided through the use of peer coaching included: 1) the ability to observe the peers coach's techniques; 2) the positive and helpful feedback provided regarding their own observed work; 3) other non-evaluative feedback; 4) the resulting reflection and ideas which they applied to their teaching; and 5) the opportunity for shared student teaching experiences. These benefits indicate possibly important implications for an inclusion of peer coaching in a teacher education program as a means to supplement supervisors' feedback.

Participants expressed difficulties scheduling peer coaching conferences and observations, which continues as an area of concern for student teachers as the peer coaching process has been instituted since this study in 2001. Recommendations to address scheduling difficulties include the need for direct assistance from university supervisors to get student teachers to allocate time for peer coaching.

An important limitation to consider is the generalization of these findings to other populations because of the small number of participants involved (N = 8) and the small size of the university. Participants were all familiar with one another and establishment of rapport was less of an issue as it might be with a larger population in a larger teacher preparation program. Increased sample size and activities to promote collegiality and collaboration would be recommendations to address these limitations.

Of critical importance, peer coaching was clearly associated with the encouragement and use of reflection. This is critical since teachers should first and foremost be able to inquire into and think critically about their teaching (O'Donoghue & Booker, 1996). A concluding remark by one participant adds powerful insight that supports peer coaching as a means to encourage reflection:

> *Peer coaching really makes you reflect on the whole lesson. It makes you think, okay what did I do and what can I do differently for the future. Also, seeing my peer's lesson, I put myself in (peer's) place and thought, okay (peer) is doing this and I am doing this in my lessons. I got to where I could almost go play-by-play; I could just rewind it in my mind and remember everything that happened.*

REFERENCES

Anderson, N., Caswell, I, & Hayes, M. (1994). Using peer coaching to provide additional feedback to preservice teachers of reading in an early field experience. *Yearbook of the College Reading Association, 16*, 211-221.

Englert, C. S, & Sugai, G. (1983). Teacher training: Improving trainee performance through peer observation system technology. *Teacher Education and Special Education, 6*, 7-17.

Garmon, A. M. (1993, April). *Preservice teachers' perceptions of the first year of a teacher preparation program*. Paper presented at the annual meeting of the American Educational Research Association, Atlanta, GA. (ERIC Document Reproduction Service No. ED 359 187).

Gormley, K. (1991, October). *Prospective teachers' perceptions about their teacher preparation and success in teaching: A preliminary analysis.* Paper presented at the annual meeting of the Northeastern Educational Research Association, Ellenville, NY. (ERIC Document Reproduction Service No. ED 342 738)

Joyce, B., & Showers, B. (1980). Improving inservice training: The messages of research. *Educational Leadership, 37*, 379-385.

Joyce, B., & Showers, B. (1981). Transfer of training: The contribution of "coaching". *Boston University Journal of Education, 16*(2), 163-172.

Joyce, B. & Showers, B. (1988). *Student achievement through staff development.* White Plains, NY:Longman.

O"Donoghue, T. A., & Brooker, R. (1996). The rhetoric and the reality of the promotion of reflection during practice teaching: An Australian case study. *Journal of Teacher Education, 47*(2), 99-109.

Showers, B. (1985). Teachers coaching teachers. *Educational Leadership, 42*(7), 43-48.

Showers, B. (1996). The evaluation of peer coaching. *Educational Leadership, 53*(6), 12-16.

BRINGING UNIVERSITY & BUSINESS GOALS

TOGETHER IN A CIS CAPSTONE COURSE

Gordon W. Couturier
University of Tampa

INTRODUCTION

The goals of the University and the needs of business (Doria et. al., 2003) for graduating seniors are met in this capstone course, the second semester of systems analysis and design courses (Dennis et. al., 2002). The courses use object oriented (Booch et. al., 1999) and Extreme Programming, XP, (Jeffries, 1999) techniques. This project oriented course provides a realistic business environment whereby students must plan, execute and control a project in a team oriented environment. In addition, problem solving and communication skills are improved by producing a working Website using Hyper Text Markup Language, HTML, and Active Server Pages, ASP, (Jupitermedia, 2003; Kalata, 2002) at the end of the course. This is accomplished through frequent presentations, generation of required documentation, participation in design/code walkthroughs, and development and execution of test plans (Pressman, 2001; Rational Process Test Plan, 2001).

COURSE CONTENT

The capstone course was developed in line with learning outcomes. By the end of the course students would be able to:

- Use the Systems Development Life Cycle (SDLC) concepts and object oriented analysis and design techniques to plan, analyze, design and implement an Internet based business system with an embedded database

- Use Extreme Programming (XP) techniques to create/modify/prioritize requirements and to produce versions of software quickly and of high quality

- Use project management skills to effectively initiate, monitor and control a project

- Participate in and lead teams

- Develop and execute unit, integration and system test plans

- Prepare, manage and document team meetings

- Participate in design and code walkthroughs

- Improve presentation and writing skills

- Develop policies and procedures that accompany a new system

- Exercise life long learning by attending a local, free technical meeting, seminar or class

BUSINESS NEEDS

Business needs are enumerated in a recent paper (Doria et al., 2003) entitled "What Business Needs from

Business Schools." These needs, and the way this course
meets them, are shown in Table 1.

Table 1
Business Needs From Business Schools

GOAL	ACCOMPLISHED BY	MEASURED BY
1. Develop "people skills" for managing effectively	Team oriented project with leaders	Team assessments by members
2. Emphasize basic skills and tools for problem solving	Project requiring use of programming, database development and project management and control	Completion of design specs, coding and testing
3. Provide strong grounding in theories of economics, measurement, governance, psychology, human behavior and leadership	Project requires frequent analysis of economic, operational and technical feasibility	All characteristics are assessed by group ratings of members of their team.
4. Learn by doing and applying multiple disciplines on the job	Project management and economic analysis used	Weekly project updates and two economic feasibilities updates.
5. Encourage electives outside traditional core curriculum	Uses economic principles for verifying economic feasibility; Web design encourages artistic abilities	Feasibility reviewed and approved; Web concepts reviewed and approved
6. Create differentiated curricula and allow concentration in specific industries	This course is the culmination of a major in Computer Information Systems.	Successful completion of course

UNIVERSITY REQUIREMENTS

The university has goals that are required to be met in the College of Business. These goals are shown in Table 2 along with the ways these goals are accomplished and outcomes are measured in the course.

Table 2
Goals Of The College Of Business

GOAL	ACCOMPLISHED BY	MEASURED BY
1. Critical thinking skills	Project (solving design And implementation problems); learn ASP & HTML	Project results (system is operational)
2. Effective speaking & writing skills	Project presentations And design documentation. Tests Are essay and problem solving only	Writings graded; presentations are required to follow a presentation scoring guide. Tests are graded on content, grammar, spelling, structure and organization
3. Interpersonal skills	Team oriented project, frequent presentations And design/code walkthroughs	Graded project with participation grades
4. A well developed value system, responsibly applied	Class discussion and test	Test essay question

5. Understanding US business enterprise in a competitive, global economy	Understanding development Of information systems to facilitate offshore development & implementation	Graded tests, project planning & control and written specifications
6. Apply broad business theories to real-world situations using computer technology as appropriate	Real world computer project to solve business problem	Graded project with required deliverables
7. Appreciation and preparation for life-long learning	Attending local conference, convention, seminar, or professional meeting (one each semester)	Attendance at local conference, convention, seminar, or professional meeting
8. Specific professional competency in functional area (Computer Information Systems, CIS)	Competency in using computers and developing applications	Tests and successful project completion (including turnover)

THE CIS CAPSTONE COURSE

The CIS capstone course is a team oriented project. Lectures are given in the first half of the course to provide the information needed by the students to complete their projects. The rest of the course is used to perform design/code walkthroughs and to review project schedules, agenda and minutes of all team meetings. Class attendance is required and there is a participation grade component to the final grade. Three times during the semester, the teams are required to submit individual team member evaluations to the instructor.

The project consists of an Internet-based project with an embedded database to give the students hands on experience in the development of business systems. They are free to choose any system they wish to develop as long as it has been reviewed and approved by the instructor in terms of complexity and relevancy.

This course is presentation and writing intensive. Students are required to present their project work at all milestones to complete the course. In this class, due to the frequency of presentations, the presentations are not graded but any serious problem in presentation skills is pointed out to the presenter. The students are given a presentation scoring tool to guide them in preparing for their presentations.

All documentation is reviewed for content, organization, structure, grammar and spelling. All tests consist of problems and essays (no true/false, fill-in the blank or multiple choice questions). The course is specified as writing intensive by the university.

The students develop schedules for iterative analysis, design, implementation, testing and delivery of their system. They perform the following:

- Review, revise and prioritize the list of user/system requirements

- Select the features to be implemented from the prioritized requirements list

- Plan two iterations of development in the 14 week semester (key Extreme Programming feature)

- Develop a user dialog for the selected features to be implemented

- Develop a prototype of the selected features' inputs and outputs

- Learn the basics of HTML and Active Server Pages (ASP and ASP.NET) since this is not covered elsewhere in the curriculum

- Design their features, produce unit and integration test plans, and perform design walkthroughs with the class

- Plan and implement user documentation and training

- Implement system and perform code walkthroughs with the class

- Test their system and present test results

- Plan and turnover their system; then continue with the next iteration of the development

Since students have very little experience in estimating and scheduling project tasks, guidance is provided in terms of which tasks are dependent upon other tasks being completed. Tables 3 and 4 show the tasks that have to be scheduled and their interdependencies. Students are allowed to change their baseline schedules at mid semester before the second iteration of analysis, design, implementation and conversion begins.

Table 3
List Of Deliverables And Grade Values
For Capstone Course

Item #	Deliverable	Points	Scheduled Date	Actual Date	Score
	DESIGN	½ for first iteration; ½ for second iteration			
1	User/System Specifications/Prioritizing	10			
2	Use Case Model	10			
3	Use Case Scenario/CRC Cards	10			
4	User Dialog	10			
5	Class Identification	10			
6	Class Relationship Diagram	10			
7	Output Specifications	10			
8	Output Prototyping	10			

9	Input Specifications	10			
10	Input Prototyping	10			
11	File Specifications	10			
12	Process Specifications	10			
13	Process Test Plans	10			
14	User Documentation Plan	10			
15	User Training Plan	10			
16	Conversion Plan	10			
	IMPLEMENTATION				
17	Database Implementation	10			
18	Process Implementation	10			
19	Primary Process Test	10			
20	Integration Test	10			
21	System Test	10			
22	User Documentation Implementation	10			
23	User Training Implementation	10			
24	Policies	10			
25	Procedures	10			

	WEEKLY REQUIREMENT				
	Agenda & Minutes	25			
	Gantt Chart Updates (Starting on week three)	25			
	Attendance/Participation	100			
	Total	400			

Table 4
Task Interdependencies Table

Item #	Deliverable	Can Be Done In Parallel With	Cannot be Completed Before
	DESIGN		
1	User/System Specifications/Prioritizing	2,3,4	-
2	Use Case Model	1,3	1
3	Use Case Scenario/CRC Cards	1,2	2
4	User Dialog	2,3	3
5	Class Identification	3,4	3
6	Class Relationship Diagram	3,5	5
7	Output Prototyping	1-4	4
8	Output Specifications	1-4	4
9	Input Prototyping	1-4	4
10	Input Specifications	1-4	4
11	File Specifications	5,6	6
12	Process Specifications	5	5
13	Process Test Plans	12	12
14	User Documentation Plan	5-12	4

15	User Training Plan	5-12	4
16	Conversion Plan	5-12	4
	IMPLEMENTATION		
17	Database Implementation	18	1-16
18	Process Implementation	17	1-16
19	Process Test	17,18	18
20	Integration Test	17,18,19	17,19
21	System Test	20	20
22	User Documentation Implementation	20,21	14
23	User Training Implementation	20,21	15
	CAN BE DONE ANYTIME		
24	Policies	All	N/A
25	Procedures	All	N/A

Due to the growth in software programming off-shore, specifications must be developed to guide off-shore programmers in their implementations. As a result, specification forms were developed for inputs, outputs, screens, files, processes and test plans that are to be designed.

The process specification ties a process together with the inputs, outputs, screens, database files and other processes with which it interacts. Another important feature of the process specification is the pseudo code for the process. This pseudo code specifies the logic of the process without actually programming it. As a result, it provides guidance to the programmer implementing the process (which may be offshore in the business world).

One of the reasons for all of these specifications is to ensure consistency and data integrity in system implementation. A data item (field, in data base terms) that is found in a file specification will probably be found in both an input specification and output specification. It is important that the definition of such an item be consistent (name, size, and type) over all of these specs or there will be an error upon implementation. This characteristic is closely watched during design walkthroughs.

When the system and user requirements are known and before the start of the design cycle, the students are required to develop the system test plan. The plan is developed at this time so that the plan will not be biased by how the system is being implemented. The plan will test both normal and error conditions.

A similar test form (with different name) is used to specify and record unit tests when object (primary) processes are designed. When more complex software modules (components) are put together from primary processes, a similar form can be used to specify and record integration tests. It is important to note that these test plans are developed during the design phase and used in the implementation/test phase of the development.

The university is located in the downtown area of a major city. Students can easily get to the convention center and hotels that host seminars, conventions, conferences and professional meetings (IEEE CS and AITP). Students are required to attend one free seminar, conference, convention or professional meeting during the semester (the instructor monitors local events and notifies students of upcoming opportunities). Students are required to turn in their meeting badges to the instructor to confirm their attendance.

Requiring attendance at one of these meetings is done to make students aware of the opportunities for free, continuing education in the immediate area. It also provides an opportunity for students to begin networking for internships while they're still in school and employment after they graduate since most graduates prefer to stay in the local area after graduation.

SUMMARY

This course provides students with a holistic, real life business situation. The iteration of the analysis, design, implementation, test and turnover of a system based upon prioritized user/system requirements gives the students the opportunity to practice Extreme Programming techniques on two occasions for a greater understanding of how modern business systems are produced.

During the analysis, design, implementation and turn-over of a system, the student is provided ample opportunity to learn and practice technological, administrative and managerial skills. Through frequent presentations and production of documents, students also exercise and improve their communication skills. By attending a local technical seminar, class or meeting, students are made aware of local free networking opportunities to stay abreast of the industry. The outcome is a student who is well equipped to participate in the fast evolving software world.

REFERENCES

Booch G., Jacobson I., & Rumbaugh J. (1999). *The unified modeling language user guide.* Reading, MA: Addison-Wesley.

Dennis A., Wixom B. H., & Tegarden D. (2002). *Systems analysis and design: An object-oriented approach with UML.* London: Wiley.

Doria J., Rozanski H., & Cohen E. (2003). What business needs from business schools. *Strategy, 32,* 2-8.

Jeffries R. (1999). *Extreme programming--An open approach to enterprise development.* Retrieved October, 2003, from http://www.xprogramming.com/xpmag/an_ open_ approach.htm.

Jupitermedia Corporation. (2003). *ASP 101.* Retrieved November, 2003, from http://www.asp101.com/.

Kalata K. (2002). *Introduction to ASP.NET, 2002.* Boston: Thomson/Course Technology.

Pressman R. S. & Associates, Inc. (2001) *Test specification: Document template.* Retrieved November, 2003, from http://www.rspa.com/docs/Testspec.html.

Rational Unified Process Test Plan, 2001. (2001). Retrieved October, 2003, from http://hep-proj-grid-fabric. web.cern.ch/hep-proj-grid-fabric/admin_procedures/docs/ others/rup.pdf.

CINEMA AS A TOOL FOR SCIENCE LITERACY

Costas Efthimiou
Ralph A. Llewellyn
University of Central Florida

INTRODUCTION

Surveys conducted by the National Science Foundation (NSF) have thoroughly documented a severe decline in the understanding and interest in science among people of all ages in the United States (NSF, 2002). About 50 percent of the people do not know that Earth takes one year to complete an orbit around the sun, that electrons are smaller than atoms, and that early humans did not live at the same time as the dinosaurs. These examples of faulty knowledge of physical sciences surely extend to life, social and literary sciences and are mirrored in other nations.

This paper summarizes an ambitious project embarked upon by the authors at the University of Central Florida (UCF) to improve public understanding of the basic principles of physical science, topics often included in the general education programs of many universities and colleges (Efthimiou & Llewellyn, 2003). This new approach, *Physics in Films*, uses popular movies to illustrate the principles of physical science, analyzing individual scenes against the background of the fundamental physical laws of mechanics, electricity, optics, and so on.

While still not a mature project, *Physics in Films* has been successful and has become a topic of wide discussion, both among UCF students and the physics education community (APS News, 2003; Chow, 2003; Graham, 2002; Grayson, 2002; Priore, 2003). Only a few similar projects have been tried earlier (Dennis 2002; Dubeck et al., 1994; Rogers, 2002). None has approached the scope of the *Physics in Films* project.

DESCRIPTION OF THE PROJECT

Genesis of the Physics in Films Project

It is our experience that students in general think that physics is difficult, hence boring, and without much relevance in their daily lives. The authors, who regularly teach physical science for non-science majors, searched for a way to instill in these students the enthusiasm and excitement that all physicists experience. After much discussion and review of existing resources (Dennis, 2002; Dubeck, 1994; Rogers, 2002), the proposal was made to accomplish this goal by adopting as a teaching vehicle a medium that students had already accepted as a reflection of today's culture. The vehicle chosen was the use of popular movies to illustrate both the basic principles and frontier discoveries of science and also to motivate students in becoming more critical observers of their world. By using popular movies as the actual mode of instruction, the intent was to provide a course in physical science that was more relevant to their daily lives and to begin to correct the many misconceptions they held about science.

Summer 2002: Action/Adventure Movies. During the summer 2002 *Physics in Films* was offered for the first time. Principles of physics were discussed using scene clips from nine popular action/adventure movies. For example, the law of gravitation as (mis)used in "Independence Day," conservation of momentum in "Tango & Cash," speed and acceleration in "Speed 2" and so on.

Figure 1 shows the nine movies used that first summer. Students were required to watch the films at home and turn in a brief, written analysis of the physics principle illustrated in each of three scenes of their own choosing (homework!). In class, five to ten percent of the class (of 90 students) were called upon each day to orally present their analysis of one scene to the class. Both the written and oral analyses became part of their grade in the course.

Figure 1
Summer 2002: Action/Adventure/SciFi Movies

Physics in Films

- Speed 2
- Armageddon
- 2001: A Space Odyssey
- The Abyss
- Tango & Cash
- Contact
- Frequency
- Eraser
- Independence day

An Example: Armageddon. As an example of how a movie clip is used in illustrating a physical principle, consider "Armageddon" (starring Bruce Willis). A huge, errant asteroid the size of Texas is on a collision course with Earth. (There are no known asteroids that large.) A team of oil well drillers is dispatched via a pair of space shuttles to intercept the asteroid, drill a hole in it at the right place, lower a large nuclear bomb into the hole, and subsequently blow the asteroid into two large pieces. The transverse velocities imparted to the two pieces by the explosion, when added to their (undiminished) velocities toward Earth, are to cause the pieces to just miss Earth, thereby averting worldwide disaster. After showing the clip, the analysis uses conservation of energy, conservation of momentum, vector addition, and the law of gravity to assess how physically realistic the solution in the film (and in such a future event) might be. The overall situation is depicted in Figure 2.

Figure 2
Asteroid Pieces Approach Earth

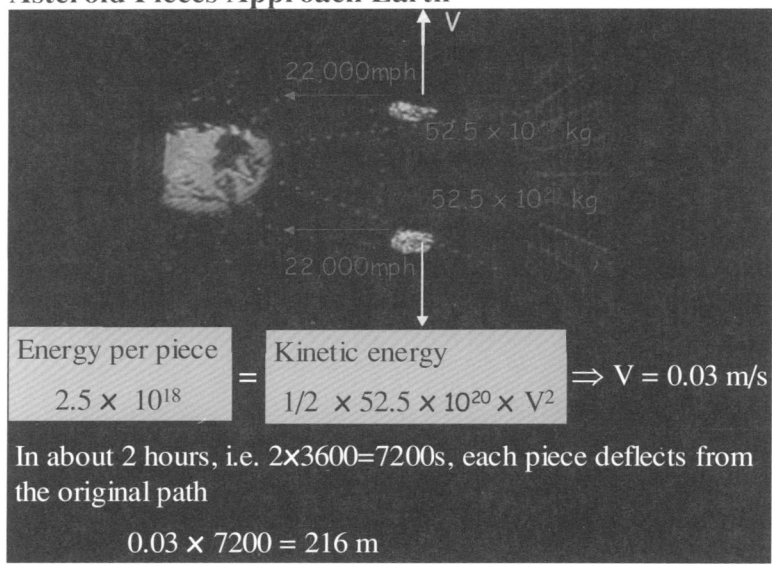

Using numbers provided in the film, the students are introduced to the idea of making reasonable approximations. For example, the asteroid is the size of Texas, so Texas is assumed to be a square whose surface area equals that of the state. Then the asteroid is approximated as a cube, each of whose sides equals the surface area of the state. Multiplying the volume of the cube by the average density of Earth gives us a decent estimate of the mass of the asteroid.

Assuming the nuclear bomb to be equal to 100,000 Hiroshima bombs provided an estimate of the energy available for the job (a modern nuclear warhead equals about 1,000 Hiroshima bombs). Assuming all of that energy became kinetic energy equally divided between the two pieces of the asteroid (i.e., ignoring the energy needed to break the asteroid into two pieces), we can readily compute the distance the pieces have moved perpendicular to their original direction of motion by the time they reach Earth. As noted in the diagram, that distance is only a bit over 200 meters for each piece.

The students are astonished. Instead of being hit by one Texas-size asteroid, Earth will be hit by two half-Texas-size asteroids about 400 meters apart! This discussion concludes with an explanation of what is realistically possible and why the government has an ongoing project to detect and track space objects approaching Earth or in Earth-crossing orbits around the sun.

Personal Response System. From the beginning all sections of *Physics in Films* have used a personal response system that enables each student to register their attendance and to record answers to questions asked in class by the instructor. The system provides immediate confirmation of answers, permits the students to change their answers, displays the correct answers, and provides a histogram of the class responses to questions so that students can compare themselves to the class as a whole.

Attendance records and responses to quiz questions, both of which contribute to the final grade, are recorded automatically by an in-class computer. The system also provides a means of recording student opinions regarding various aspects of the course, information that is helpful in improving the presentations. For example, Figure 3 contains two tables showing student responses to the use of the system itself. Shown, too, in the picture are a few communication pads like the ones used by individual students.

Figure 3
Rating the Electronic Response System

 Rating of the Electronic Response System

The electronic response system was a benefit for the class.

Summer 2002: class of 92 students.

SA	A	D	SD
28.57%	42.86%	15.58%	12.99%

Fall 2002: class of 292 students.

SA	A	NO	D	SD
44.75%	27.40%	7.76%	6.39%	13.70%

SA=Strongly Agree; A=Agree; NO=No Opinion; D=Disagree; SD=Strongly Disagree

Development of Flavors

After *Physics in Films* had been given for three terms to four sections with a combined enrollment of about 800, the improved performance of the students relative to the traditional physical science course together with their enthusiasm regarding the *Physics in Films* approach motivated the authors to explore new directions for developing the course further. The original syllabus included movies selected to span the entire topical range of the traditional physical science course. No special attention was given to the genre or theme of the films used. The films eventually used, like those in Figure 1 for the first term, were action/adventure, and science fiction films.

Encouraged by the students' enthusiasm, the authors considered possible variations of the course that would accommodate the curiosity of every student and satisfy the needs of every instructor. It was decided to create versions (packages)—nicknamed "flavors"— whereby each flavor used films of a particular genre or theme. Plans have been developed to create the following flavors: Action/Adventure, Science Fiction, Superhero, Modern Physics, Astronomy, Pseudoscience, and Metaphysics. During the summer and fall 2003 terms the Superhero and Pseudoscience flavors were given for the first time.

Physics in Films: Superheroes. Part of the motivation for offering the Superheroes flavor came for a course given by Jim Kakalios at the University of Minnesota-Twin Cities (Feder, 2002). He has taught a successful course in physical science based on superhero comic books. The *Physics in Films: Superheroes* flavor complements Kakalios' approach, substituting motion and 'real' action for static images. It was first taught in the summer 2003 term using the films shown in Figure 4.

Figure 4.
Physics In Films: Superheroes Films

   Physics in Films: Superheroes

- Superman I, II, III, IV
- Batman
- Batman Returns
- Batman & Robin
- Batman Forever
- Spiderman
- X-Men
- Daredevil
- X2
- The Hulk

When the course was in progress, two of the films ("The Hulk" and "X2") were not yet available on disk or tape, so the students had to go to the theatres, but no one complained. In fact, the whole class approved!

The topical content of *Physics in Films* originally closely followed that of traditional physical science courses. The textbook was "Fantastic Voyages" (Dubeck et al., 1994). While somewhat 'lighter' than a typical physical science textbook, it uses some (rather old) movies as illustrations and is the only such text available. In *Physics in Films: Superheroes* classes however, the authors deviated somewhat from the traditional path and added some decidedly non-traditional books. They were "The Science of Superheroes" (Gresh & Weinberg, 2002), "The Science of Superman" (Woolverton, 2003), and "The

Science of XMen" (Yaco & Haber, 2000), all illustrated in Figure 5. Stocked in the trade book sections of the bookstores, they are replete with applications of the concepts of physical science. The authors of these books frequently use physical laws in an effort to make the powers of the superheroes plausible to the lay reader. In so doing they provide fertile ground for lively discussions.

Figure 5.
Physics in Films: Superheroes books

An Example: "Spiderman." As an illustration of a superhero film in the course consider "Spiderman" (starring Tobey McGuire) and a specific scene. The scene is where the Green Goblin is standing on one of the towers of the Queensboro Bridge in New York simultaneously holding Mary Jane (MJ) suspended over the river with his left hand and the broken cable holding the Roosevelt Island cable car filled with children with his right hand. This one scene provides for discussions in equilibrium of forces, torque, friction, and free fall. Considering the latter, the Green Goblin presents Spiderman, who is crouched on the bridge superstructure, with a dilemma by allowing both MJ and the cable car to fall. Which will Spiderman save?

Timing events directly from the film clip, students see that it takes Spiderman 14 seconds to decide and start after MJ first, saving her, then saving the children in the cable car. It looks great in the film! But when the instructor leads the students through analysis of MJ's fall they discover that in those 14 seconds she would fall a distance $d = \frac{1}{2} g t2$ where $g = 9.8$ m/s2 and $t = 14$ s. Thus, $d = 960$ meters and the Queensboro Bridge is only 106 meters above the water! Once again, the students are astonished! Even assuming that the director implies `slow motion' effects as he presents the events, we can estimate that Spiderman cannot react and catch MJ in less than 5 seconds. This would give a free-fall length of 122.5 meters, still more than the height of the bridge.

    Physics in Films: Pseudoscience.   An idea or theory is called pseudoscience if it contradicts accepted scientific data, but is presented as scientific. Note that a mistake or error in presenting scientific data does not signal pseudoscience. It is the intentional misrepresentation of facts or unverified claims that justify the label. For our purposes the authors categorize as pseudoscientific those movies that are based on topics or phenomena that contradict scientific facts. There are many such films that might be used, but a group was chosen that most students had already seen or knew about. (See Figure 6.) *Physics in Films: Pseudoscience* was first taught in the summer 2003 term.

Figure 6.
Films used in Physics in Films: Pseudoscience

 Physics in Films: Pseudoscience

- The Others
- Independence day
- Sixth Sense
- Clockstoppers
- Unbreakable
- The Crucible
- Practical Magic
- The Craft
- Sleepy Hollow
- Harry Potter
- Signs
- Dragonfly

The topics covered and related to pseudoscience included, among others:

- o Universality of physical laws – magic
- o Time – time reversal, time stopping
- o Strength of materials – unbreakability
- o Chemical reactions – zombies
- o Fundamental interactions – ghosts
- o Intelligent life in the universe -- alien visitors to Earth, alien abductions

Figure 7
Books used in Physics in Films: Pseudoscience

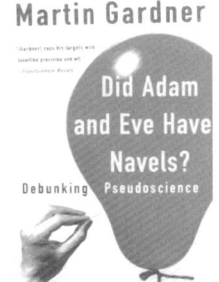

An Example: The Sixth Sense. Among the topics discussed in physical science are the related concepts of temperature and heat transfer via conduction, convection, and radiation. "The Sixth Sense" (starring Bruce Willis) is concerned with ghosts. The movie tells us that ghosts like low temperatures, although why that should be is not made clear.   In the scene where the young hero goes to the bathroom during the night, a sudden drop in temperature is clearly shown. We have been told that this heralds the appearance of a ghost, and indeed one appears.

As it happens, a scientific study of this presumed phenomenon has been done (Frood, 2003). The Haunted Gallery of Hampton Court Palace near London, UK, is reported by many visitors to be haunted by the ghost of Catherine Howard (fifth wife of Henry VIII, executed in 1542). Air motion and thermal detectors were deployed in the Gallery and some 400 visitors were asked about their experiences during the visit. More than half felt sudden drops in temperature, some sensed ghostly presence, and several reported seeing Elizabethan figures. The study (Frood, 2003) revealed many poorly sealed hidden doorways that admitted columns of colder exterior air. In two locations the temperature of the localized draft was only 36° F!

A Course Book Display. The UCF campus bookstore cooperated by installing a prominent display 'island' featuring the *Physics in Film: Superheroes* and *Physics in Film: Pseudoscience* courses (Figure 8). The display attracted student attention and (the authors suspect) increased sales of the displayed books, as well.

Figure 8
UCF Bookstore display for Physics in Films

ASSESSMENT AND FINDINGS

As of this writing, the *Physics in Films* alternative to the traditional Physical Science course has been offered at UCF since the summer 2002 term to a total of nine sections enrolling, collectively, about 1600 students. During that time the authors have collected data regarding student evaluations of the course and their performance on exams. In that same time period there have been seven sections of Physical Science taught in the standard way, enrolling about 2000 students.   Some of the more interesting results and comparisons are presented in this section.

Examination Results

Even though students may embrace a new idea enthusiastically, that does not mean their performance will necessarily improve relative to the traditional course (where most of them really struggle). Student performance on individual exams and overall are improved in the *Physics in Films* sections when compared with those in traditional Physical Science sections. Table 1 shows the exam scores distribution for two classes of about the same size (295 students each), covering the same topics, and taught by the same instructor. The results are obviously dramatically different!

Table 1
Comparison of Exam Results

Instructional Mode	Exam 1	Exam 2	Exam 3	Final Exam
Traditional Class average percent	49.3	65.3	58.2	59.4
Physics in Films Class average percent	74.9	67.7	75.7	72.8

Student Evaluations and Opinions

Since Physics in Films was first offered, considerable data has been collected regarding student opinions and evaluations of the course and the various flavors taught to date. This section summarizes some of the more interesting of those data.

Table 2
Responses to the Statement: *Physics in films should be developed further since it is more interesting than the standard physical science course.*

Term No. of students	Strongly Agree	Agree	No Opinion	Disagree	Strongly Disagree
Summer 2002 92	77.9%	10.4%	n/a	9.1%	2.6%
Fall 2002 292	56.9%	26.6%	6.9%	4.1%	5.5%

Table 3
Response to the statement: *I think I learned something from this class (Physics in Films: Superheroes).*

Strongly Agree	Agree	No Opinion	Disagree	Strongly Disagree
60%	32%	5%	1%	2%

Table 4
Responses to the statement: *I would recommend to my friends that they take this course (Physics in Films: Pseudoscience).*

Strongly Agree	Agree	No Opinion	Disagree	Strongly Disagree
68%	25%	5%	2%	0%

Table 5
Responses to the statement: *The topics selected from the movies for physics analysis were interesting.*

Strongly Agree	Agree	No Opinion	Disagree	Strongly Disagree
42%	42%	16%	0%	0%

However, changing the public's overall perception of science is not easy. More and longer term efforts reaching a much broader audience will be needed. As Table 6 suggests, fear and unreasonable dislike of science are deeply rooted in the minds of students and others, as the NSF surveys cited in the introduction to this paper makes clear.

Table 6
Responses to the statement: *I do not like science and I do not want to read anything about science once I have finished this course.*

Strongly Agree	Agree	No Opinion	Disagree	Strongly Disagree
25%	26%	8%	18%	23%

CONCLUSIONS AND RECOMMENDATIONS

It appears clear from the information and data presented herein that the *Physics in Films* alternative to the more traditional Physical Science course captures student interest and improves their performance.   Approximately half of the students who enroll in Physical Science at UCF now take the *Physics in Films* version, a further testament to the success of the approach.

The Future

The authors will certainly continue their work at UCF in further developing the *Physics in Films* concept. However, it may be argued that will not be enough. As Table 6 and the NSF surveys have made clear, changing public perceptions of science will be neither easy nor quickly accomplished.

It is the goal of the authors to increase the awareness of science and to show that an understanding of basic physical science can be both enriching and rewarding. To this end they are working toward the development of 'packaged' *Physics in Films* flavors that can be readily transferred to other institutions. They are also writing a new physical science textbook designed to support the *Physics in Films* mode of teaching. In addition, they have begun to explore the application of the concept to the creation or enhancement of general education courses in many other disciplines. List 1 presents several possibilities together with a few examples of films that include material for each discipline.

List 1
Extensions to Other Disciplines

- ❖ **Mathematics in Films:** *Pi, Good Will Hunting, Pay it Forward, Contact*

- ❖ **Astronomy/Astrophysics in Films:** *Armageddon, Deep Impact, Contact*

- ❖ **Biology in Films:** *Spiderman, The Hulk, Planet of the Apes, Jurassic Park*

- ❖ **Chemistry in Films:** *Flubber, Year of the Comet*

- ❖ **Engineering in Films**: *Armageddon, The Bridge on the River Kwai*

- ❖ **Archeology/Anthropology in Films:** *Indiana Jones trilogy, Jurassic Park*

- ❖ **Computers in Films**: *The Net, Independence Day, War Games*

- ❖ **Philosophy in Films:** *Blade Runner, Matrix, Terminator trilogy, Ghost*

- ❖ **History in Films**: *Braveheart, Patriot, The Man in the Iron Mask*

- ❖ **Law in Films**: *Erin Brockovich, The Firm, Legally Blond, Primal Fear*

- ❖ **Forensic Science in Films:** *Jennifer 8, Murder by the Numbers, Bone Collector*

REFERENCES

APS News(2003). *Physics in films*. Retrieved January 6, 2004 from http://www.aps.org/apsnews/0303/030306.html.

Chow, L. (2003). Cinema as physics lesson. *Physics Today*, *56*, 15. Retrieved January 6, 2004 from http://www.physicstoday.org/vol-56/iss-5/p15a.html.

Dennis, C.M., Jr (2002). Start using "Hollywood Physics" in your classroom. *Physics Teacher, 40,* 420.

Dubeck, L. W., Moshier, S. E., & Boss, J. E. (1994). *Fantastic voyages: Learning science through science fictions films*. New York: Springer.

Efthimiou, C. E. & Llewellyn, R. A. (2003*). Physical science: A revitalization of the traditional course by avatars of Hollywood in the physics classroom*. Retrieved January 6, 2004 from http://www.arXiv.org/physics/0303005.

Feder, T. (2002). Teaching physics with superheroes. *Physics Today, 55,* 29.

Frood, A. (2003, May 21) *Ghosts 'all in the mind'*. London: BBC News. Retrieved January 6, 2004 from http://news.bbc.co.uk/1/hi/sci/tech/3044607.stm

Graham, A. (2002). *A little bit of Hollywood, a lot of physics*. Retrieved January 6, 2004 from http://www.ucffuture.com/main.cfm?include=detail&storyid=328832.

Gresh, L. & Weinberg, R. (2002), *The science of superheroes*. New York: Wiley.

Grayson, C. (2002). *Students play games, watch movies, raise grades.* Retrieved January 6, 2004 from http://www.ucffuture.com/main.cfm?include=detail&storyid=328832

NSF (2002). *Science & engineering indicators 2002.* Retrieved January 6, 2004 from   http://www.nsf.gov/sbe/srs/seind02.

Priore, T. (2003). *With great power comes a physical explanation: Action films teach students the laws of physics.* Retrieved January 6, 2004 from http://www.ucffuture.com/news/main.cfm?include=detail& storyid=436180

Rogers, T. (2002). *Personal communication.*

Woolverton, M. (2003). *The science of Superman.* New York: BP Books.

Yaco, L., & Haber, K. (2000). *The science of XMen.* New York: BP Books.

DELIVERING INTERNET-BASED

MATHEMATICS HOMEWORK

USING WEBWORK

Jason Farmer
Coreen Mett
Neil P. Sigmon
Radford University

INTRODUCTION

One of the major factors currently limiting the success of students in mathematics courses is their inability to spend the appropriate time needed on homework. This factor coincides with the surveys taken from Radford University's incoming freshman that indicated that 78 % spent fewer than five hours per week during their high school senior year engaged in academic activity outside of class.

To alleviate this problem, the mathematics department at Radford University, through the support of a National Science Foundation grant (DUE project 0125586), has integrated the Internet-based homework system WeBWorK fully into all sections of college algebra currently being offered. Originally designed by Professors Michael Gage and Arnold Pizer at the University of Rochester with support from the National Science Foundation, this program is currently being employed by many colleges and universities in courses ranging from high school algebra to the calculus sequence and beyond.

The purpose of this paper is to describe the features of WebWorK and its integration into Radford's mathematics curriculum. More details concerning the implementation of this work at Radford University can be found at the project Website illustrated by Farmer and Mett (2003a). A more detailed explanation of WeBWorK can be found at the Website illustrated by Gage and Pizer (2003b).

INTERACTIVE STUDENT LEARNING

A well-known factor for success in mathematics courses involves student willingness and motivation to work homework problems that reinforce concepts that are taught in class. One of the major strengths that WeBWorK provides is a strong interactive learning environment from which students can easily accomplish this task. Some of the features that make this possible are described below.

Easy Accessibility and Simple to Learn

WeBWorK is an Internet-based homework delivery system. Students can access WeBWorK using any computer with access to the Internet. To access WeBWorK, students are given an initial user identification and password that allows access to his or her private account. A private account for each student resides at the course Website.

WeBWorK is easy for students to use and learn. The syntax for entering answers in WeBWorK is similar to the syntax required to enter numerical quantities and mathematical formulas on most graphics calculators. Figure 1 given below illustrates an example homework problem with questions and typical answers.

Figure 1
WeBWorK Problem Example

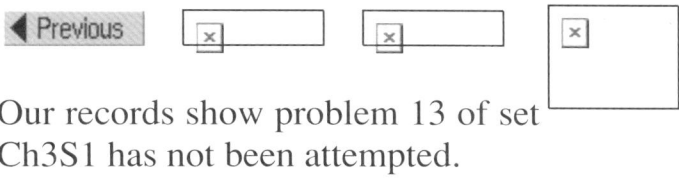

Our records show problem 13 of set
Ch3S1 has not been attempted.

Top of Form

(1 pt) setCh3S1/setch3s1n47-48.pg

Below is the graph of the function f : (Click
on the image for a larger view). You should
note that the grid lines represent 1 unit on
the larger view. Use the graph to answer the
questions below.

Determine   f(0) = -5   ,   f(5) = 8   ,
f(-7) = 0

Indicate whether the following functional values are
positive, negative, or zero.

1. f(□2)
2. f(4)

In interval notation, state the domain of f. NOTE: If the answer includes more than one interval, write the intervals separated by the "union" symbol, U. If needed enter ∞ as infinity and –∞ as -infinity.

domain = | [-7, 8] | .

List the values of x (separated by commas - no parenthesis or brackets!) representing the x intercepts

x intercepts = | -5, 1, 7 |

| Submit Answers | Preview Answers |

WeBWorK has the ability to record the work an individual student has completed on an assignment. This gives the student the flexibility to be able to partially work an assignment, logoff, and then reconnect back to WeBWorK and not lose any of the assignment that was previously completed.

Instant Feedback

When an answer to a problem is submitted, WeBWorK provides instant feedback on the correctness of the problem. When a mistake occurs, a student has the opportunity to correct the problem. The instant feedback motivates the students to spend the time necessary to get the problem correct. Comments from students include:

WeBWorK assignments are extremely helpful to me because it shows me what I get` wrong and allows me to work out the answer until I get it correct. This is effective for me

WeBWorK is very effective. I really like how you can keep doing the problem until you get it right. It gives you a chance to understand the problem

Students normally attempt a problem as many times as they wish until the due date of the assignment. The instructor does have the option of limiting the number of allowed attempts, which can be beneficial when asking matching and true false type questions.

Because of WeBWorK's ability to assign random coefficients in each problem, each student receives a unique problem from the same general concept. This factor makes WeBWorK excellent for group learning, since students can solve problems together by discussing the mathematical concept without being able to copy each other's work.

INSTRUCTOR INTERACTION
IN THE LEARNING PROCESS

WeBWorK gives the instructor the ability to easily manage a course and to interact with students in the learning process. On each problem page, students have a feedback button that will send an e-mail message directly to the instructor. This allows the student to communicate with the instructor directly on the particular problem that is giving difficulty. Instructors can quickly view the precise problem an individual student is working, along with the most recent student entry, which allows easy interaction by e-mail, telephone, or in person with each student.

The size of the class does not restrict the instructor in student interaction or in managing the course. WeBWorK instantly grades each student's assignment. The grades are easily downloaded onto a spreadsheet that can be quickly recorded. WeBWorK has great flexibility on administering individual homework. Assignment due dates can be extended to an individual student without extending the due date to the entire class. Flexible mechanisms are available for evaluating symbolic and numerical answers. This allows the students to enter answers in different formats that are correct.

Instructors have access to more than two thousand problems that are available at the University of Rochester website library covering topics ranging from high school algebra to the calculus sequence and beyond. Instructors also can create their own problems using a combination of the programming language Perl and the mathematics typesetting language LaTeX, both of which can be understood in a short period of time.

WEBWORK AT RADFORD UNIVERSITY

Currently, WeBWorK is being administered to all sections of college algebra, which is a general education course taken each semester by over 400 students. Normally, part-time adjunct instructors teach most sections. At the beginning of each semester, a workshop is provided to introduce new faculty to WeBWorK.

Feedback has been very positive, both from students and instructors. Figure 2 shows a histogram that represents the number of students, from a sample college algebra class, who attempted a certain number of WeBWorK assignments. For example the chart demonstrates that 15 students attempted all eleven WeBWorK assignments. The color-coded bar represents the grade students received from course (4 represents the number who received an A, 3 represents the number who received a B, etc.). The graph clearly illustrates a definite correlation between student success and the number of WeBWorK assignments that were attempted.

Figure 2
Correlation between Student Success and WeBWorK Assignment Attempts

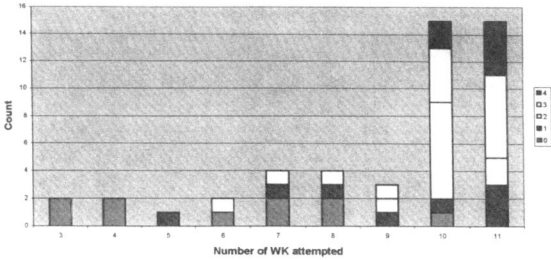

SUMMARY AND CONCLUSIONS

As mentioned above, WeBWorK has been fully integrated into all sections of college algebra at Radford University. Many new problems suited for college algebra have been written and tested. The positive response received from students and instructors is similar to that found at other institutions that currently use WeBWorK. To continue this success, the department is in the process of integrating WeBWorK into the first two semesters of the calculus sequence. Several members of the mathematics department have voluntarily used it in other selected courses, including business calculus and finite mathematics.

Long term plans for WebWorK include making it available for inclusion in the local high school curriculum, specifically targeting Algebra II. WeBWorK will be an integral part of the mathematics department's quality enhancement plan for increasing student engagement. In summary, WeBWorK will continue to be a valuable tool for increasing student motivation, engagement, cooperative learning skills, and developing positive attitudes towards mathematics.

REFERENCES

Farmer, J., & Mett, C. (2003). *Radford University WeBWorK: Course site*. Retrieved November, 2003 from http://webwork.radford.edu.

Gage, M, & Pizer, A. (2003). *WeBWorK Meliora Mathematica University of Rochester University: Course site*. Retrieved November, 2003 from http://webwork.math.rochester.edu/.

PREPARING TEACHERS FOR THE PRESENT
AND THE FUTURE

Pedro F. Hernández-Ramos
Santa Clara University

INTRODUCTION

This article describes some of the efforts undertaken at a small liberal arts university with a long history of teacher preparation to evolve at all levels, from structural (becoming a department in a new School, formerly a program in a Division) to strategic (e.g., hiring new faculty, creating new MA programs), and tactical (e.g., increasing the availability of technology within the department). Three options, labeled Mobility, Real World, and Virtual, have been explored in some depth. A greater availability of technology and concurrent pedagogical changes are expected to position the department and its programs in a favorable situation, to succeed as it faces some foreseeable challenges and others that inevitably will crop up unexpectedly.

THE RECENT PAST

The Department of Education at Santa Clara University is in its third year of operations (starting in 2000) under that name, although the university had operated a teacher preparation program under a Division of the College of Arts and Sciences for over twenty years. Only in 2003 was a new School of Education, Counseling

Psychology and Pastoral Ministries created to split the three departments from the College, and a new Dean appointed.

As a department, three new faculty have been added, the teacher preparation program has been revised to conform to new state guidelines (it did conform to the old ones), new Masters programs have been created, and significant changes in policies and procedures have been implemented or are in process.

The author joined the faculty in 2001 to focus on educational technology in the teacher preparation program and to direct a new MA emphasis in "Teaching and Learning with Technology." At that time the department did not have any of its own technology resources—no computer lab, no software of particular use to future teachers (e.g., educational titles focused on subject matter areas like math or language arts), and a very limited history of technology integration in any of the courses in the teacher preparation sequence. In addition, the department faced serious constraints in facilities, since the university had limited classroom space and no short-term prospects for new buildings that could alleviate these problems.

Partly in response to these challenges and partly as a strategy to address long-term goals and needs, three different though complementary technological and pedagogical options are being implemented—*Mobility*, *Real World*, and *Virtual*.

THE MOBILITY OPTION

Towards the end of the 2001-2002 academic year, the department obtained an internal grant to purchase a mobile laptop computer cart. Equipped with 16 laptops, all capable of wireless connectivity, a wireless access point, and a laser printer, the cart gave Education faculty the option of turning any existing classroom into a technology-equipped "lab," with no additional investments required from either the University (which already had all classrooms wired with Ethernet ports) or the department.

The positive impact on the teacher preparation program was felt immediately in the only course in the sequence ("Instructional Technology for Teachers") focused on technology integration, and has had small but noticeable benefits in other courses (including the Methods courses) where access to the laptops, software, and the Internet improves the teaching and learning experience. For example, in a Math Methods course the instructor was able to have the students use a CD-ROM with case studies that helped preservice students who had no access to field settings see how special needs children could benefit from differentiated instruction (De La Paz, Hernández-Ramos, & Barron, in press).

In Language Arts and Reading courses, instructors have identified Websites for the students to explore and study as sources of information and reference. And in the "Instructional Technology for Teachers" course, students were able to learn software applications that will help them with their communications, personal productivity, teaching preparation, and learning needs. Other activities included time to explore rich resource Websites like the Library of Congress (www.loc.gov) and international collaboration projects like the Global Schoolhouse (www.globalschoolnet.org), among others.

THE REAL WORLD OPTION

For future K-12 teachers, learning about technology integration in a university classroom is a major exercise of the imagination. Most of them have spent very little time in classrooms, and even as they begin to experience classrooms on a daily basis as part of their teacher preparation experience, the vast majority of them report not seeing practicing teachers integrate technology in any meaningful way—if they use it at all— even for personal productivity at school.

In the summer of 2002, and again in summer 2003, a decision was made (Hernández-Ramos & Giancarlo, in press) to move the "Instructional Technology for Teachers" course from the university classroom out to "the real world"—a local technology-rich elementary school with a Teacher Development Center located on its premises. After working out the agreements with the district and the school, two sections of the course were delivered as intensive one-week workshops that ran for 6 hours each day (compared to two hours once a week for ten weeks).

Location is a factor in learning that educational institutions sometimes conveniently ignore. It is easier for students to congregate in a "place of learning" (e.g., school, university) and expect them to acquire knowledge, facts, information, attitudes, and skills that they should later be able to apply in the so-called "real world" outside. When the expectations fail, education institutions tend to place the responsibility with students (it is they who "fail" to "apply what they learned") rather than critically examine the process.

Herrington and Oliver (1999) compiled a list of "nine characteristics of a situated learning framework, namely: an authentic context; complex authentic activities; multiple perspectives; expert performances; coaching and scaffolding; opportunities for collaboration, reflection and articulation, and authentic assessment" (p. 402). Our course was designed with the goal of meeting all these criteria.

Situating the course at the elementary school and Teacher Development Center was possible because the school had adequate technology available for staff development purposes. Also, most or all of the teachers at that school were "master" technology-using teachers. By allowing the interns and pre-service student teachers to visit on-site classrooms and observe these teachers in their daily practice, these master teachers served as role models that, in the best case, made it easy for student teachers to convince themselves that they, too, could teach with technology. These ideas were further addressed in scheduled conversations during the workshop week, where master teachers and the school principal (a former teacher at the same school) shared their personal and professional stories.

Co-teaching was modeled in this course by the two university faculty and site coordinator leading it. Teaching is usually a profession where individuals do not collaborate on a regular basis. Multiple reports (Dwyer, Ringstaff, & Haymore Sandholtz, 1990) and other research argue for increased collaborations among K-12 teachers (Fontaine, 2000), and yet few teacher preparation institutions are actively addressing this goal in their curricula and in the practices of their faculties. If it is true that "teachers teach the way they were taught," modeling co-teaching in this course will likely encourage future teachers to work collaboratively when their time in the classroom arrives.

For pre-service students, the time lag between exposure and practice, the difference in context of instruction versus context of practice, and the perceived relevance of what's learned in the university classroom versus what will be needed in the "real" classroom are among the most salient (Milken Exchange on Educational Technology, 1999). In this course experience the department aimed to address several of the shortcomings at once. The overarching goal for this course—and for the program in general—has been to improve on the fact that "only 20 percent of teachers feel well prepared to integrate education technology into classroom instruction" (CEO Forum on Educational Technology, 1999, p. 10).

For pre-service students in particular, having the class in a school with adequate facilities, led by faculty who model effective use of technology, being able to observe teachers who can serve as good models, learning computer applications with clear connections to practice (and time to explore them on their own), seeing elementary students relate to technology with ease and confidence, and working on a meaningful project for later use in their own classroom form a set of critical conditions. Obviously, the short time of the experience (five days) is not enough to convert students into full-fledged, sophisticated, technology-using teachers. Longer sessions (e.g., summer institutes lasting three to five weeks) and ongoing support increase the comfort levels, proficiency, and likelihood of sustained use of technology (Ringstaff, Yocam, & Marsh, 1996; Sandholtz, Ringstaff, and Dwyer, 1997).

THE VIRTUAL OPTION

One advantage of the quarter-long course framework is that it allows some activities that are not practical in a week-long, intensive workshop setting. In the Spring of 2003 the "Instructional Technology for Teachers" course was offered on campus, one day a week, two hours each session, for ten weeks. Course activities for the 56 enrolled students (split into two sections) included creation of a Web log ("blog") using the free version of Blogger.com and to e-mail the instructor with the resulting URL.

Blogs and Online Discussion Boards

The assessment rubric for the course specified that to gain full credit for this component students had to do "10 or more postings 1-paragraph or larger" during the quarter in their blogs, starting in week three (out of 10), on the broad subject of "teaching, learning, and technology." The rubric also specified that students had to join in an online discussion board (within the university's Prometheus course management system), which was available only to people participating in the course (each section had its own online discussion area). The instructor posed three discussion questions during the quarter, and the rubric asked for "timely and insightful" participation.

The lack of a "voice" in daily professional practice is just one of many issues confronting teachers, and a factor in the usually low job satisfaction ratings contributing to the very high proportion (almost 50 percent) of new teachers who abandon the profession within the first five years of practice (NBC17.com News, 2002). Part of the challenge for a teacher preparation program is how to inculcate in graduates a greater sense of the importance of their profession, how to see themselves as producers of information and knowledge, and not "just as teachers" who are solely in a transmission role.

More significantly, teacher preparation programs must encourage students (future teachers) to claim their professional voice and the means to be heard. The possibility that technology can be a factor to address these problems and meet these goals is evident, for example, in the National Educational Technology Standards (International Society for Technology in Education, 2002) that include under the category of "Productivity and Professional Practice" the following goals:

> Teachers use technology to enhance their productivity and professional practice. Teachers
>
> • Use technology resources to engage in ongoing professional development and lifelong learning.
>
> • Continually evaluate and reflect on professional practice to make informed

decisions regarding the use of technology in support of student learning.

• Apply technology to increase productivity

• Use technology to communicate and collaborate with peers, parents, and the larger community in order to nurture student learning. (p. 306)

The University of Santa Clara teacher preparation program in particular places a great emphasis on reflective practice and social justice issues, so providing meaningful mechanisms for students to engage in active reflection with a reference to larger social issues are key goals. Many courses in the program require students to maintain a journal, so the use of blogs and online discussions was consistent with past practices, supported the ISTE standards for teachers, and introduced technology-based tools in a meaningful way (Jonassen, Peck, & Wilson, 1999).

Given the above two vehicles for self-expression and reflection, students had the opportunity to consider the differences between a "public" venue addressing an unknown audience (the blogs) and a more "private" option where all participants were known to each other. A complementary goal was to encourage students to see both blogs and discussion forums as valid and effective tools for professional development and lifelong learning.

For online discussion forums, the three topics launched by the instructor elaborated on ideas and issues addressed in the readings and during class sessions. They were separated by about a three-week period each, giving adequate time for the students to post their initial reply and then come back to reply to a peer's posting.

The first discussion, posted on the third week of the quarter, read as follows: "Read the story titled 'Browser revolution–10 years after' available both as a PDF file in Prometheus and ERes (the university's electronic reserve system) and on the Web at: http://zdnet.com.com/21001104 -996652.html. If you read it online, check the discussion forum at the end of the story. After reading the story, respond to these two questions: 1) Do you see any impact of the Internet in the schools you know? Where? How? and 2) How would your life, both personally as a current or future teacher, be different if you didn't have access to the Internet and to the we in particular?"

The second discussion, posted at the end of the fifth week, was: "What do you think? The use of productivity applications as learning tools…(Example: Producing a classroom newsletter with your students using a word processor)."

The third and final discussion was launched at the beginning of the ninth week and asked: "What is an online learning community? Can we learn from our professional peers through online interactions? Are there some topics or skills that are better suited to the online medium? What would motivate you to become an active participant in an online learning community?"

There were two key ideas behind the use of blogs and discussion forums for their online reflection. The first was that the "conversations" implied in the personal journal are expanded beyond the intrapersonal (the student with her/himself) and dyadic (student/instructor) to include—in the case of blogs—a potentially large and unanticipated audience.

Feelings of ambivalence and even anxiety cropped up. One student wrote:

> *I'm definitely not into the blogging thing yet. It feels very weird to me to be writing for an unknown audience, and at the same time it is not private.*

The second goal relates to the fact that this and other students have trouble seeing themselves as active creators of knowledge, or at least, as budding professionals whose ideas are worthy of consideration by others. For example, one student wrote:

> *I feel like I am adding to the useless information out on the Web. There are different tools, like Prometheus* (the online discussion forum environment), *that I think I would use.*

By making their reflections public via blogs and visible to their peers in the discussion forums, students are contributing to the general social discourse and their audience is no longer only the instructor. From a pedagogical perspective, the expectation is that the quality of what is written and published on the blogs and discussion forums will be of higher quality, an insight corroborated by experience and some research (Norton & Wiburg, 2003). Furthermore, by becoming comfortable with the idea of publishing their writing either to the world or to an online community, there are reasons to hope that these future teachers will be motivated to engage their own students in projects such as online newspapers or Websites that will also make visible the students' work (Serim and Koch, 1996).

The use of blogs and online discussion forums in the same course fulfilled several pedagogical and learning goals. At one level, the experience was designed to increase awareness in the students about differences in electronic communication tools and environments. At another level, one goal was to help students develop a sense of themselves as creators of knowledge, rather than just consumers of information, and to see themselves as meaningful contributors to professional dialogues. At yet another level, their participation in the course's online community (the discussion forum) suggested the idea that their student peers could be seen as valuable sources of information and ideas, a connection that ideally they will carry past their graduation date.

Moving Toward Electronic Portfolios

Increasing the availability of technology resources for Education students is part of a larger strategy to allow the department to change and adapt to important trends in the field and to meet demands from state agencies overseeing teacher preparation institutions. Grant funds were obtained from a private foundation to create an "Electronic Portfolio Laboratory" for the Department of Education, equipped with top-of-the-line computers, scanners, digital video and photo cameras, an extensive software library, and a high-end server to support (among other services) ample storage space for students as they begin to build electronic portfolios containing a variety of digital (or digitized) products as an integral part of their teacher preparation experience.

Teachers are increasingly being encouraged to record, evaluate, and present information electronically, comfortably manipulating the virtual world of media and digital images. Although books and printed materials continue to be the staple in K-12 classrooms, credential candidates in a growing number of California teacher preparation programs are required to maintain a record of their achievements in the form of a media-rich electronic portfolio (Bartlett, 2002).

Kovalchick, Milman, and Elizabeth, (1998) defined electronic portfolios as follows:

A technology portfolio is similar to a traditional portfolio, but it specifically addresses technology skills and issues. Also, the medium is different since it is organized using a combination of electronic media such as hypermedia programs, database, spreadsheet, and word processing software, as well as CD-ROMs and the World Wide Web. Technology portfolios can be print-based, saved in a computer disk, compiled on a CD-ROM or HomePage, or a combination of the above. (p. 4)

Innovations in teacher preparation encourage the use of technology to express knowledge and demonstrate pedagogical skills. While enrolled in the Department of Education, credential candidates will be able to create one or more of the types of portfolios commonly used (Wolf, 1999). These include Learning portfolios, where candidates have an "an opportunity to explore, extend, showcase, and reflect on their own learning" (p. 12); Assessment portfolios, where candidates select and compile course work for analysis and evaluation by teachers and peers, though the "primary purpose" is usually "to evaluate teacher performance for certification licensure, or professional advancement" (p. 13); and Employment portfolios, designed to communicate to prospective employers the candidate's abilities and professional interests.

Created by student teachers, these electronic documents (available on the Web, or assembled in CD-ROMs or DVDs) will provide future employers with a better sense of what credential candidates know and how they teach. They offer a rich alternative to paper student records, grade reports, and course listings.

CONCLUSIONS

Becker (2000), and Willis and Sujo de Montes (2002) are examples of research pointing to the fact that future teachers who are meaningfully exposed to and work with technology as part of their teacher preparation experience are more likely to integrate it into their own practice. The three options explored in depth in this paper—Mobility, Real World, and Virtual—are complementary efforts to enrich the teacher preparation experience through the meaningful integration of technology.

Mobility is the option that acknowledges the larger trend in computing toward smaller yet full-featured machines capable of doing most or all of the tasks possible with a desktop computer (e.g., video editing, which requires significant processing power), and allow users to accomplish others that are impossible with desktop computers (e.g., work in multiple locations with full access to all of one's information). The implications for the design of learning environments in schools and classrooms, for example, are now beginning to be realized in the building of new schools that support wireless connectivity throughout, letting teachers, students, and administrators access teaching, learning, and administrative tools and resources with much greater convenience than before.

Santa Clara University Department of Education's plan is to explore the possibility of providing preservice students with laptops and/or PDAs (personal digital assistants). It is envisioned that such tools will help them produce and collect materials and information for their electronic portfolios, to serve as agents of influence at the schools where they are placed during their preparation process, and to become increasingly comfortable and knowledgeable with technology tools to increase personal productivity and effectiveness as teachers and lifelong learners.

The *Real World* option recognizes the influence of Brown, Collins, and Duguid's (1989) path-breaking work on situated learning. The author's own experiences moving one course from the university classroom to a school setting (Hernández-Ramos & Giancarlo, in press) clearly indicate that students benefit significantly from guided observations in authentic settings and from learning technology applications with the purpose of integration into practice.

Beyond the placements at schools that the students are already involved in, the intention with the technology course is to have different sections for multiple subjects and single-subject students (K-5 and 6-12 in most cases), since the elementary school setting used so far is not as advantageous to the single-subject candidates as it is for the multiple subject candidates. Other courses, particularly during the summer session, have begun to explore moving all or a significant number of the class sessions to a local school setting. This will allow the preservice students the opportunity to work with real students in authentic settings which usually is more productive and rewarding for everyone.

The *Virtual* option leverages the power of electronic communication tools to develop not only students' communication skills, but also their own powers of reflection, interaction with peers in disparate locations through online communities, and their self-image as professionals with a voice and perspective that deserves to be heard and recognized. Careful ongoing analyses of students' blogs and postings in online discussions, and the products carefully assembled into an electronic portfolio can yield valuable insights for instructors. For example, it may be possible to identify students who need support with writing, analytical skills development, or motivation "…to tackle challenging tasks and help them acquire a deep level of understanding" (National Research Council, 2001, p. 281).

Like other traditional forms of journaling, both blogs and online discussions afford the instructor and peers opportunities to get to know each other better. Many students who are shy in person and whose voices are rarely heard in the classroom are capable of presenting themselves through their blogs and of assuming vibrant personas in online discussions enriching the conversations in ways that they don't seem able to do during in-person class sessions. Students who have much to offer also benefit from having online tools through which their ideas and experiences are shared with all without dominating conversations in the classroom.

The next step in the Virtual option is to advance the conversations within the university toward serious consideration of "distance learning." The current course management system available on our campus can support students from anywhere in the world so long as they have an Internet connection. Currently the university is not formally considering offering courses online, although there are signs that this is something that several graduate programs will need to offer in the near future in order to remain competitive.

In the Department of Education, the Electronic Portfolio Laboratory, in addition to exposing future teachers to new ways to teach and learn, will transform student teachers from simple consumers of knowledge created by others into reflective practitioners and active collaborators who create and share new knowledge, building a dynamic community of professionals that goes beyond the preservice experience and extends into their professional practice. The implementation of the portfolio process also presents challenges and opportunities for the faculty, since our own levels of use of technology—and understanding of the power and possibilities of the tools available to us—has to increase accordingly.

REFERENCES

Bartlett, A. (2002). Preparing preservice teachers to implement performance assessment and technology through electronic portfolios. *Action in Teacher Education 24*(1), 90-97.

Becker, H. J. (2000). *Findings from the Teaching, Learning, and Computing Survey: Is Larry Cuban right?* Retrieved December 30, 2003, from http://epaa.asu.edu/epaa/v8n51/.

Brown, J. S., Collins, A., & Duguid, P. (1989). Situated cognition and the culture of learning. *Educational Researcher 18*, 32-42.

CEO Forum on Educational Technology. (1999). School Technology and Readiness Report. *Professional development: A link to better learning.* Retrieved October 17, 2002 from: http://www.ceoforum.org/reports.cfm?RID=2.

De La Paz, S., Hernández-Ramos, P. F., & Barron, L. (In Press) Multimedia environments in mathematics teacher education: Preparing regular and special educators for inclusive classrooms. *Journal of Technology and Teacher Education.*

Dwyer, D. C., Ringstaff, C., & Haymore Sandholtz, J. (1990). *Teacher beliefs and practices Part II: Support for change. The evolution of teachers' instructional beliefs and practices in high-access-to-technology classrooms. First-fourth year findings.* [ACOT Report #9.] Cupertino, CA: Apple Classrooms of Tomorrow.

Fontaine, M. (2000). Supporting teachers with technology: Don't do today's jobs with yesterday's tools. *TechKnowLogia*, November/December, 14-16. Retrieved October 2, 2002 from http:// www.TechKnowLogia.org.

Hernández-Ramos, P. F., & Giancarlo, C. A. (in press). Situating teacher education: From the university classroom to the "real" classroom. *Journal of Computing and Teacher Education.*

Herrington, J., & Oliver, R. (1999). Using situated learning and multimedia to investigate higher-order thinking. *Journal of Educational Multimedia and Hypermedia, 8*(4), 401-421.

International Society for Technology in Education. (2002). *National educational technology standards for teachers. Preparing teachers to use technology.* Eugene, OR: Author.

Jonassen, D. H., Peck, K. L., & Wilson B. G. (1999). *Learning with technology. A constructivist perspective.* Upper Saddle River, NJ: Merrill Prentice Hall.

Kovalchick, A., Milman, N. B., & Elizabeth, M. (1998). *Instructional strategies for integrating technology: Electronic journals and technology portfolios as facilitators for self-efficacy and reflection in preservice teachers.* (ERIC Document Reproduction Service No. ED421115).

Milken Exchange on Educational Technology. (1999). *Will new teachers be ready to teach in a digital age? A national survey on information technology in teacher education.* Santa Monica, CA: Milken Family Foundation.

National Research Council. (2001). *Knowing what students know. The science and design of educational assessment.* Washington, D.C., National Academy Press.

NBC17.com News. (2002). *More teachers leaving profession early.* Retrieved July 31, 2003 from http://www.nbc17.com/news/1790906/detail.html.

Norton, P., & Wiburg, K. M. (2003). *Teaching with technology. Designing opportunities to learn* (2nd ed.). Belmont, Ca: Wadsworth.

Ringstaff, C., Yocam, K., & Marsh, J. (1996). *Integrating technology into classroom instruction: An assessment of the impact of the ACOT teacher development center project.* (ACOT Report #22.) Cupertino, CA: Apple Classrooms of Tomorrow.

Sandholz, J. H., Ringstaff, C., & Dwyer, D. (1997). *Teaching with technology—creating student-centered classrooms.* New York: Teachers College Press.

Serim, F., & Koch, M. (1996). *NetLearning: Why teachers use the Internet.* Sebastopol, CA, O'Reilly & Associates.

Willis, E. M., & Sujo de Montes, L. (2002). Does requiring a technology course in preservice teacher education affect student teacher's technology use in the classroom? *Journal of Computing in Teacher Education* *18*(3), 76-80.

Wolf, K. (1999). *Leading the professional portfolio process for change.* Arlington Heights, IL: Skylight Professional Development.

BLENDING TECHNOLOGY

INTO REVIEW SESSIONS

Jessica Herron
Roy P. Pargas
Clemson University

INTRODUCTION

For many students the pen and notebook typically found in their backpacks are now augmented by their digital counterpart: the laptop computer. Not only are students able to perform many classroom activities electronically, but they can reach beyond the classroom to the Internet via wireless networking connections. Several universities have instituted mandatory laptop programs. While these programs are not the focus here it is important to understand the widespread implementation of laptop technology.

Clemson University began a pilot laptop program for 100 freshmen in the Fall of 1998. In the Fall semester of 2003 over 4000 freshman, sophomores and juniors will enroll in laptop classes in varying subjects (Campbell & Pargas, 2003; Clemson University, 2003; Moss, 2000). The wireless network at Clemson covers many common areas for students as well as an ever-growing number of classrooms. Other universities with similar laptop mandates are the University of North Carolina, University of Florida, Mississippi State University and Colorado State University.

The next question, of course, is: *How are instructors using this new tool?* There are many examples of booming technology with high expectations that flop in the classroom. In a study of classroom use of technology since 1920, Cuban (1986) observed a specific cycle that classroom technology follows from its inception to its dissolution. He concluded that the ultimate failure of a classroom technology was rooted in the lack of adequate instructor integration (Cuban, 1986; Oppenheimer, 1997). This is the current challenge—how to incorporate technology productively into the classroom. The answer appears to lie not in the technology itself, but in the teaching methods. Instructors need to adapt pedagogy to take advantage of the benefits that technology provides.

One aspect of teaching that can benefit from new technology is the student teacher question and answer interaction. This bi-directional communication occurs in two instances—students clarifying their understanding of the material or teachers evaluating their students understanding.

The first instance of this student-teacher communication is like a review session, the objective of which is to give students an opportunity to ask questions to gain more understanding (such as before a big exam). For clarity, any reference to this kind of student-teacher interaction will be considered a review session. The second instance of this student teacher communication occurs on a more regular basis where teachers pose questions to their students to gage how well the students comprehend the information. For clarity, references to such student-teacher interactions will be considered student polls.

The typical model of these interactions usually involve a classroom of students, an instructor, and a chalkboard. This model works if the instructor is before a relatively small number of students with pens and notebooks. The model is less effective in a large lecture hall full of students and fails completely if students and instructor are not necessarily in the same room. In such a situation and if the students have access to computers, technology can help. The Clemson Online Review

Environment (CORE) leverages the benefits of electronic communication in its support of pedagogy for the laptop classroom.

BACKGROUND

There is a large amount of research that supports the use of technology and computer mediated communication in the classroom. Grabe (2001) outlines several advantages. He notes that computer mediated communication's biggest advantage is its impact on student participation. In a typical classroom, almost all communication occurs between instructor and student rather than among students. While this is often desirable, there are instances in which interactive learning and student collaboration can enhance learning.

Supporters of collaborative learning claim that the active exchange of ideas within small groups not only increases interest among the participants but also promotes critical thinking. One study (Johnson & Johnson, 1986) found that cooperative groups achieve higher levels of comprehension and retain information longer than students who work alone. There is also evidence that traditional instruction tends to involve those students who dominate the conversation. Students who can develop fast responses monopolize the instructor's attention (Althaus, 1997).

Creed (1997) documents his experience of electronicizing his class. He lists several key advantages to online education, of which four are relevant: accessibility, pedagogy, thoughtful discussion, and a level playing field.

The first advantage refers to the increased accessibility by the student to important information. Documents and notes stored in specially designated directories and folders are immediately accessible to all students in a class. The number, physical well-being, and geographical location of the students cease to be issues.

A second advantage of electronic communication is its potential to improve pedagogy. In most classes there is a broad spectrum of student abilities and backgrounds. Studying and reviewing online allows students to choose their own paths. Regarding the online hypertext format, Creed says, "The student is in control of what information comes her way, and at what pace. Such a technology has always been the goal of designers of teaching machines, and the web provides it" (Creed, 1997, p. 62).

A third advantage of electronic communication is its ability to provoke thoughtful discussions. Creed points out that students craft their questions much more thoughtfully through the written medium than they do in oral conversations. The absence of non-oral communication requires that the student's written message be very clear and well thought-out. Finally, a fourth advantage of electronic communication is that it levels the playing field for all students. An online system allows quieter students to participate equally with their more boisterous classmates.

CLEMSON ONLINE REVIEW ENVIRONMENT

Clemson Online Review Environment (CORE) directly capitalizes on these advantages. It is an online system, which allows students to actively participate in an open dialogue with their classmates and instructor or Teaching Assistants through the Internet. This applies to both review sessions and student polls. This benefits students absent, but can also benefit students in the room in several significant ways.

Accessibility

Not only can students submit questions to their instructor, but they can read questions in previous review sessions. In a regular review session students write down information and forget to actively listen to the information being presented. In CORE, because the information is electronically recorded, students can pay attention to the instructor and understand her/his message without being distracted by note taking. Students can access all of the information that transpired in class or in the review from anywhere on the Internet. The accessibility is not only recognized by the student, but by the teacher as well. Many professors find themselves balancing their role as instructor with their role doing research and attending conferences. This flexibility allows instructors to access their students' questions and concerns and address them from any where on the Internet.

Pedagogy

Through its search capability, the Clemson Online Review Environment allows students to elicit what information they would like to learn more about. If they have a question on a specific topic, they can read other postings on that topic. But if they understand a topic, they do not have to spend any more time with it. This "student-centered" review is a much more effective and efficient use of a student's time. They can also keep track of all the questions they've posted and are notified when the instructor has answered the question. This is one of the main advantages that CORE has over other classroom collaboration tools such as WebCT.

Thoughtful Discussion

The Clemson Online Review Environment gives the students a chance to think about their questions and word them exactly as they want. Instructors also get the advantage of written communication. It allows instructors to continuously update answers they have posted. In a regular review session an instructor may forget to say something important with regard to a question. With CORE s/he can update it at any time and the information is available for all to review. The review session evolves into a living session instead of something that occurred, and can continue at the teacher and students convenience.

Level Playing Field

The Clemson Online Review Environment allows students to voice their thoughts invisibly. A future function is to give the student an option to remain anonymous to all reviewing students. The instructor can see who asked the question, but to the rest of the class, the student remains anonymous. CORE also enables quieter students to develop their own thoughtful responses to questions by submitting follow-up remarks to another student's pending question.

Inexpensive Option

While there are other software packages such as WebCT and Blackboard that have similar functionality, CORE is free to the Clemson University community. It was developed with the Computer Science curriculum in mind, but is scalable to all faculties of the university.

MPLEMENTATION OF THE
CLEMSON ONLINE REVIEW ENVIRONMENT

CORE is written in Java (version 1.4) and utilizes Java Beans accessed by Java Server Pages (Sun's Java, 2003). Java Beans allow the developer to cleanly package the computational sections code into well-organized and logical groups. Java Server Pages, on the other hand, provide powerful tools for presentation of content. This clean separation of content from format facilitated the development of CORE significantly. The HTML pages generated are served by Apache's Tomcat servlet engine (version 3.2.3). Behind the scenes, the system accesses an Oracle database (version 9i) which holds all information, including userids, questions, answers, URLs of images, and access frequency counts. Currently CORE is not available for general download or use. If the system is ported to MySQL there is a better chance this system will be more widely available for licensing reasons.

User Views

After logging on and selecting a course, a student is presented with two sets of review sessions associated with the course, one labeled active and the other inactive. A review session is active if the instructor has left it open for student questions or answers. An inactive review is still available to the student but in read-only mode. After selecting a review session, the student is presented the session view (Figure 1), which consists of three panels. On the left is the question panel, which lists the subject lines of questions that have been posted, ordered by their current status. The middle panel is the information panel where instructions are provided, a question and the instructor's response may be viewed, and the student may enter follow-up answers or comments. The right panel is the active users' panel, which shows the list of users currently logged into this active review session.

Figure 1
CORE session view

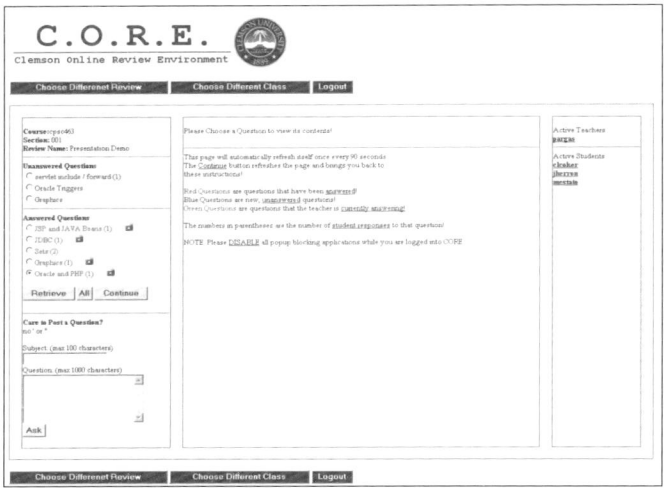

Questions

A question has three parts: the question itself, the instructor's answer, and follow-up answers or comments from students.   A question is entered through the left panel of the session view (Figure 1).   The status of a question is "Unanswered", "Currently being answered", or "Answered" and is denoted as such by certain colors. Students quickly know where the instructor is in answering questions.

An instructor can post an answer to any question by first retrieving it and then attempting an answer. A media component (still image, audio, or video) may be associated with the answer through a URL reference (Figure 2). CORE includes the component in the answer whenever it is viewed.   An instructor may, for example, draw a diagram as part of an answer on a whiteboard and capture the image with a Webcam attached to her computer. The image is associated with the answer in real time.

Figure 2
Enlarged view of CORE session

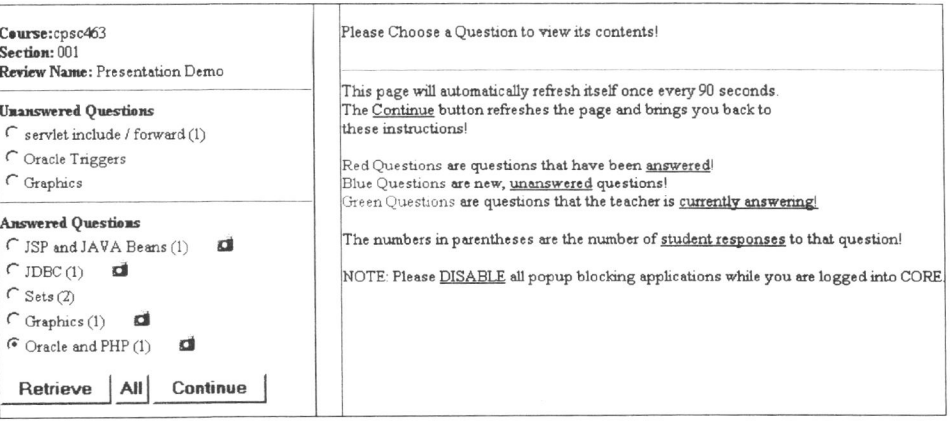

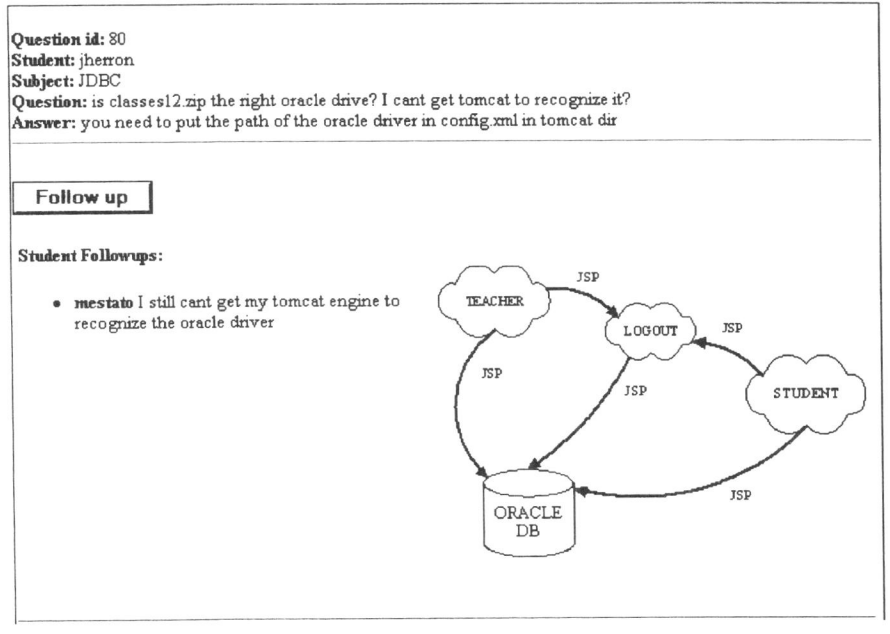

To harness the potential of a collaborative environment, students are able to post a follow-up (comment, answer, or another question) to any question. The number of follow-ups is in parenthesis next to the subject lines of the questions in the left panel of the session view (Figure 1). A follow-up allows students to enter their own answers to the question, expand upon a previous answer, or request more information if they still do not understand the answer. This function not only allows students to be actively involved in each others' learning, but helps the instructor better understand specific student problems. That some students learn best when they try to teach others was a motivation for the development of this function.

Along with asking and answering questions, CORE allows a student to search all of the previously posted questions by keyword. This function returns a list of questions that contain the search keywords provided by the user. This is helpful for students who are having difficulty in one topic area. This saves time for both the instructor and the student. If someone previously asked about Oracle JDBC drivers and an adequate answer was provided the student need not post a new question.

Instructor Specific Tools

In addition to most of the student functions, instructors are given additional privileges that help them administer review sessions. From the course view, an instructor can update a class roll which determines which students have access to a specific course. An instructor can create a new review or reactivate an old one. Instructors have ultimate administrator rights over the content in the Clemson Online Review Environment. They can delete reviews and questions and disassociate questions from a review. Instructors can delete an entire review. This does not delete the questions that were associated with it—it simply erases the review container.

Both instructors and students have the ability to search CORE. This function returns a list of questions that contain the keywords specified. Instructors have the additional ability, after receiving the results of their search, to select a subset of questions either to add them to another review or to create a new review from the questions selected. This is a key function for instructors as they can save time answering a question that has previously been answered either in a different review session or an entirely different class. Questions are part of a review by association. One question can be associated to several different reviews.

Experience with CORE

The first version of CORE, completed in early summer 2003, was used in a relatively small (16 students) summer course offering of CS4: Data Structures and Algorithms. All lectures and labs were conducted by the instructor in a computer lab room equipped with desktop computers. A graduate teaching assistant was also present at all lectures and labs. Lectures were taught in mentoring, coaching, or studio mode, characterized by reduced lecture and increased student collaborative in-class activity.

The following review sessions were conducted (prior to tests) in the three different styles listed below.

Non-electronic. The instructor and students were together in one room. The instructor answered questions orally and drew diagrams on a whiteboard.

Electronic. the instructor conducted a 1-1/2 hour review session from Seattle, WA while the students were in Clemson, SC (not all in the computer lab room). A graduate assistant was with the students and participated by interjecting clarifying remarks about students' questions.

Hybrid. The instructor and students were together in the computer lab room and the first 30 minutes of a review session were spent communicating through CORE. The students entered questions and follow-ups and the instructor answered questions, all in silence. This was followed by another 30 minutes of non-electronic, oral review.

Near the end of the summer session, an informal assessment of the three review sessions was conducted by group discussion. A summary of the discussion is described below.

CORE is again being used in a CS4 course during the Fall 2003 semester. This class has 68 students and is designated as a laptop class, that is, each student must have a laptop computer with wireless access to the campus network and the Internet. The instructor and two graduate assistants meet with the students in two weekly 75-minute lecture sessions and one 110-minute lab session.

Lecture sessions start with a 10-minute online quiz (using WebCT), a 20-40 minute lecture supported by online notes, applet animations, and PowerPoint presentations, The room is large and populated with 15-foot tables rather than desks, facilitating instructor-encouraged student collaborative activities. The space between tables is large enough for the instructor or the teaching assistants to pass in order to answer a question of a student at the end of a table.

Because the class size is moderately large and students are all laptop-equipped, most communication outside of class is conducted through e-mail and postings on the class Website. Few students have made use of the twelve office hours (divided among the instructor and two graduate students) sprinkled throughout the week. And trying to arrive at a single hour outside of class time when the instructor and all students were available for a review session turned out to be impossible. In this course, CORE is essential and indeed the only practical way that a review session can be conducted. The instructor uses it extensively for real review sessions as well as in class activities. This is discussed further in Summary and Future Work below.

EVALUATION OF CORE

Near the end of the Summer 2003 CS4 course, the instructor and students assessed CORE through group discussion. The student opinions held by the majority or significant plurality are summarized below:

Non-electronic

Advantages. Highest rated:

- Face-to-face meetings and oral response to questions with the use of a whiteboard offer the greatest benefit to students attending

- Students can interrupt an instructor's explanation and ask for clarification on a specific point

- The instructor can focus on and emphasize key points more easily helping the students understand better the relative importance of issues

Disadvantages. On the down side:

- Only students physically present benefit

- No record, other than individual student notes, is available after a session

- Only questions asked during the session are answered. Some students claimed that they had questions but could not attend the session and were not able to give their questions to students who could

Electronic

Advantages. Highest rated:

- Having a review session with the instructor before a test is better than not having a review session. (The instructor was attending a conference and a test was administered by a teaching assistant in his absence.)

- Questions and answers are saved by CORE and are available after the session to all students, including those who do not attend.

- Students can also participate by providing answers to questions and reaction comments.   This helps both the student who can clarify her/his thoughts as well as the instructor who, from reading the comments and students answers, can better understand the root causes of misconceptions.

Disadvantages. On the down side:

- Communicating entirely through a keyboard is awkward at best and discourages some students, particularly those who cannot type well, from asking detailed questions.

- A Webcam or a tablet is not easy to use to draw diagrams. Considerable practice with these devices is required, particularly when responses are being generated in real-time.

- Because students are keying questions into CORE simultaneously, the instructor at times is too busy answering primary questions and fails to notice and answer follow-up questions. Several such questions remained unanswered at the end of the session and the students who asked them were disappointed.

Hybrid

The students concluded that there were no unique advantages or disadvantages to the hybrid review session since each 30-minute session was identical to either the electronic or non-electronic sessions. The discussion, however, led to what they felt would be the ideal review session, characterized as follows.

- The instructor should allow students to enter questions into CORE before a scheduled face-to-face meeting and, if possible, the instructor or teaching assistant should answer the questions in CORE before the meeting.

- The instructor should assign one or more students either from the class or among the teaching assistants to serve as scribes. The task of the scribes is to take notes (manually or electronically) and to enter the questions and answers into the system. The entry need not be performed in real-time, but should be performed immediately after the review session in order to benefit students who could not attend.

- Whenever appropriate, digital snapshots of the whiteboard should be taken and the digital images should be associated in CORE with the corresponding questions and answers.

SUMMARY AND CONCLUSIONS

The instructor plans to use CORE in future classes and to conduct recitation, or class participation. The reason is that the room being used is large and cavernous, with a 40-foot ceiling, and capable of accommodating 140 students comfortably. It is impossible for students to project their voices loud enough for everyone to hear and use of the whiteboard at the front of the room is worthless. However, the projector is powerful and works well to provide a wide-screen display of the instructor's laptop screen.

The plan is for the instructor to ask a question, entered before class into CORE, and to solicit responses from students. Each student's response will be recorded in the system as a follow-up to the question and can be projected on the screen for general discussion and comment. This, the instructor believes, is a perfect way to critique, for example, segments of code written by students. To preserve student privacy, the instructor will project from a dummy student account which will cause the system to mark some students' responses simply as "Student".

The number of laptops continues to grow in many colleges and universities. While this expansion is important, it is also important for teaching methods to develop and evolve as well. The next phase of this project will also include careful monitoring of CORE usage by students and a study as to whether there is any correlation with final grades. Usage monitoring is already built into the system and such a study would be relatively straightforward.

REFERENCES

Althaus, S. L. (1997). Computer-mediated communication in the university classroom: An experiment with online discussion. *Communication Education, 46*, 158-176.

Campbell, A. B., & Pargas, R. P. (2003, April). *Laptops in the classroom.* Thirty-Fourth SIGCSE Technical Symposium on Computer Science Education, Reno, NV, 98-102.

Clemson University. (2003) *Wireless at CU*. Retrieved July 15, 2003 from http://www.clemson.edu/networkservices/Wireless/wireless.htm.

Creed, T. (1997). *Extending the classroom walls electronically*. Edina, MN: Interaction Book.

Cuban, L. (1986). *Teachers and machines: The classroom use of technology since 1920*. New York: Teachers College Press.

Grabe, M. (2001). *Advantages and pitfalls of computer-mediated communication*. Grand Forks, ND: University of North Dakota.

Johnson, R. T., & Johnson, D. W. (1986). Action research: Cooperative learning in the science classroom. *Science and Children, 24*, 31-32

Moss, W. (2000, February). *Developing and implementing a pilot laptop program*. UCF-Dell Laptops in the Classroom Conference. Retrieved January 7, 2004 from http://www.math.clemson.edu/~bmoss/developC.htm.

Oppenheimer, T. (1997). *The computer delusion*. Retrieved July 15, 2003 from The Atlantic Online http://www.theatlantic.com/issues/97jul/computer.htm.

Sun's Java. (2003). Retrieved July 15, 2003 from http://www.java.sun.com.

Note: The authors wish to thank the Clemson University students of CPSC 212-1, Summer 2003 for their thoughtful comments and suggestions regarding the use of the Clemson Online Review Environment (CORE).

ALTERING ACHIEVEMENT MOTIVATION

TO ENHANCE CLASSROOM LEARNING

Mark Sudlow Hoyert
Cynthia D. O'Dell
Indiana University Northwest

INTRODUCTION

It is a truism that motivation is important to learning. While every teacher believes this, nobody has been able to map out the exact linkages between motivation and classroom performance. The best practical advice that generally can be offered is that more motivation is better. However, this might not be true. Rather, it might be the case that multiple varieties of motivation exist and that even moderate levels of some varieties may be more adaptive than high levels of others.

GOAL ORIENTATION THEORY

One psychological theory concerned with the relation between motivation, learning, and classroom performance is called Achievement Motivation or Goal Orientation theory (Ames & Archer, 1988; Dweck & Leggett, 1988; Harackiewicz, Barron, & Elliot, 1998; Hidi & Harackiewicz, 2000). Goal orientation theory suggests that when students engage in a class, they strive to reach one or more goals. Some students want to satisfy a requirement. Other students are interested in the material. Some have heard that this is an easy class.

Goal Orientation theory suggests that two goals are of primary importance— *mastery goals* and *performance goals.* Students who adopt mastery goals are interested in learning the material in the class and strive to master that material (Ames, 1992; Blumenfeld, 1992; Dweck & Leggett, 1988). Students who pursue performance goals are interested in demonstrating their competence, especially relative to other students (Dweck & Leggett, 1988; Urdan, 1997).

Mastery and performance goals are multidimensional motivational constructs. That is, these goals provide a framework through which a variety of behavioral, cognitive and affective responses are energized and directed (Ames, 1992; Blumenfeld, 1992; Dweck & Leggett, 1988). For instance, research under a variety of laboratory and classroom settings has found that students who pursue mastery goals display a wide variety of largely adaptive behaviors and attitudes not seen in all students. Mastery oriented students seek to improve their competence through acquiring new skills and knowledge and by surmounting novel and difficult problems.

Mastery goals have been found to be associated with increased interest, the enjoyment of challenge and challenging tasks, and the belief that competence is obtained incrementally through effort. Students who pursue mastery goals commonly use effective learning strategies such as elaboration and organization, have developed multiple strategies, are interested in developing new skills, become involved in the learning process, display greater persistence, and are likely to respond to challenges through the use of greater effort and the exploration of alternative learning strategies (Albaili, 1998; Ames, 1992; Ames & Archer, 1988; Blumenfeld, 1992; Elliot & Harackiewicz, 1994; Graham & Golan, 1991; Harackiewicz, Barron, Carter, Lehto, & Elliot, 1997; Harackiewicz, Barron, Tauer, Carter, & Elliot, 2000; Harackiewicz & Elliot, 1998; Pintrich, Zusko, Schiefele, & Pekrum, 2001).

The pursuit of performance goals is more complex, but sometimes has been associated with a less adaptive set of academic outcomes such as self-aggrandizing, task aversion, the pursuit of effort minimizing strategies, a reluctance to seek help, impaired problem solving, greater feelings of self-consciousness, self-handicapping, and helplessness.   Students who adopt a performance goal orientation seek to elicit favorable judgments of their competence and avoid negative evaluations.   These individuals tend to prefer and to seek out easier tasks where success and validation can be obtained and view competence as static and unaffected by effort. The maladaptive behaviors are more likely to appear when validation is not available (Albaili, 1998; Dweck, 1999; Dweck & Leggett, 1988; Graham & Golan, 1991; Harackiewicz, Barron, & Elliot, 1998; Harackiewicz, Barron, Tauer, Carter, & Elliot, 2000, Harackiewicz & Elliot, 1993; Kong & Hau, 1996; Midgley, 1993; Pintrich & Schunk, 1996; Pintrich, Zusko, Schiefele, & Pekrum, 2001; Ryan, Gheen, & Midgley, 1998; Somuncuoglu & Yildirim, 1999; Urdan, Kneisel, & Mason, 1999; Urdan & Maehr, 1995; Urdan, Midgely, & Anderman, 1998).

The adoption of mastery goals should be associated with academic accomplishment. In the college classroom this would translate into better examination and course grades and a higher grade point average. One would expect that a mastery-oriented student who monitors comprehension, connects new information with old, can discriminate more important information from less important information, who sets goals, uses elaboration and other adaptive learning strategies should attain higher levels of academic success than a performance oriented student who procrastinates and self-handicaps.

In contradiction to the above, however, most studies employing an objective measure of academic performance in the classroom have not found a consistent or robust advantage. Only a third of the studies have reported higher grades for mastery-oriented students (Bouffard, Boisvert, Vezeau, & Larouche, 1995; Eppler & Harju, 1997; Pintrich, Zusko, Schiefele, & Pekrum, 2001; Schraw, Horn, Thorndike-Christ, & Bruning, 1995; Wolters, Yu, & Pintrich, 1996) and about two thirds have obtained null results (Beck, Rorer-Woody, & Pierce, 1991; Elliot & Church, 1997; Greene & Miller, 1996; Harackiewicz & Elliot, 1998; Harackiewicz, Barron, Carter, Lehto, & Elliot, 1997; Harackiewicz, Barron, Tauer, Carter, & Elliot, 2000; Harju & Eppler, 1997; Pintrich & Garcia, 1991; Pintrich & Garcia, 1993; Roedel & Schraw, 1995). *No studies have found that pursuing mastery goals is associated with declining academic success.*

THE CURRENT STUDY

A New Hypothesis

These above studies have all examined goal orientation and grades in an undifferentiated set of students under typical classroom conditions. Dweck (1999) has speculated that the goal orientation effects are altered or amplified during stress or challenge but she has never examined this prediction.

In the current study, the authors identified an obvious and frequent source of stress in students— failure on a test. They therefore examined the effects of goal orientation after failure on an examination. Students were tracked to see what happened on the subsequent examination after the failure. Students who endorsed mastery orientation had a 15 point increase on the next examination. Students who pursued performance goals had a 10 point decrease. Not only did different patterns of goal orientation lead to an effect on academic performance, but it was very robust. A 25 point difference in examination scores can lead to a difference of two or three letter grades. Further, ninety-five percent of the mastery oriented students attained a higher examination grade on the subsequent test. About half of the performance oriented students had a decrease in test grade on the subsequent examination (Hoyert & O'Dell, 1999, April; 2000, May; 2001, April; 2001, May; in press; O'Dell & Hoyert, 2000, April; 2002, May).

Thus, it appears that Goal Orientation is very relevant to academic success. In particular, it seems to have a strong effect following a challenge. Performance-oriented students struggle following a failure while mastery orientation seems to better prepare students to face that challenge.   As a result, the authors began exploring an intervention to aid struggling Introductory Psychology students. The intervention is designed to increase mastery orientation, prevent the failure effect seen in performance oriented students, and increase academic success.

Method

Instruments. Goal orientation was measured using Roedel, Schraw, and Plake's (1994) Goals Inventory. This instrument consists of 25 statements rated on a 5-point Likert-type scale for strength of agreement. Students were asked to consider how much each of the statements applied to themselves within the Introductory Psychology class. The statements assess attitudes and behaviors towards learning and performance goals as described by Dweck and Leggett (1988).

Procedure. During the first day of the semester and at the final examination, the goal inventory was administered to all students. The study involved three groups of participants— the intervention group, a control group matched for initial examination grade and goal orientation and who did not receive any tutoring, and a group who received academic tutoring. Following the first examination, all students were invited to voluntarily participate in one of the tutoring groups. Students who were performance oriented and had failed the examination were contacted outside of class and encouraged to attend. At the end of the academic term, the students' introductory psychology examination and course grades were obtained from the instructor.

Within the intervention sessions, peer tutors and students engaged in a variety of activities, all aimed at increasing the adoption of mastery orientation. The techniques included orientation modeling from several different perspectives, discussion of multiple study techniques, goal setting, and value referencing. It must be pointed out that the tutorials only addressed motivational issues. They did not cover classroom material. Within the academic tutoring sessions, peer tutors discussed content from the lecture and textbook and explored practice tests. These activities were designed to increase the acquisition of knowledge and did not have a motivational component. Each session lasted 45 to 60 minutes.

Results

Sixty-four students participated in the motivational intervention and 40 students participated in the academic tutorial. The two groups combined comprised about 20% of the target students.

As can be seen in Figure 1, the intervention produced an increase in endorsement of mastery goals. At the onset of the semester, students in the intervention, control, and tutorial groups had lower mastery goal scores than the average Introductory Psychology student (class M=3.557; intervention M=3.174; control M=3.193; tutorial M=3.257). Over the duration of the semester, the students in the intervention group increased their endorsement of mastery goal orientation (intervention; M=3.370, t(63)=3.904, p<.001). Mastery goal orientation remained constant for the other two groups (control M=3.210, tutorial M=3.250).

Figure 1
Mean Goal Orientation Scores

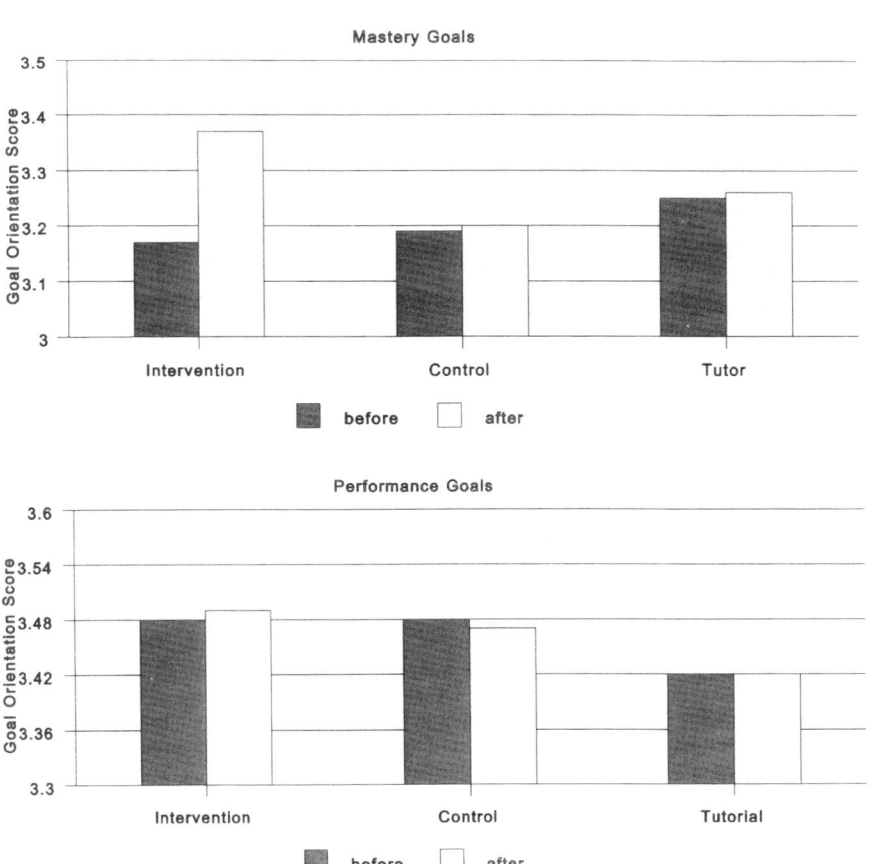

At the onset of the semester, all three groups of participants had similar performance goal orientation scores (class M=3.41; intervention M=3.476; control M=3.481; tutor M=3.417). Performance goal orientation remained constant for all three groups over the semester (intervention M=3.485; control M=3.466; tutor M=3.419).

Examination grades improved following the intervention and after academic tutoring. In the intervention group, the mean examination score increased from 57.67 to 66.15 ($t(63)=5.333$, $p<.001$). For the tutoring group, the mean scores increased from 58.25 to 62.15 ($t(39)=2.602$, $p=.013$). The grades decreased for the control group from 57.72 to 54.56 ($t(63)=-2.778$, $p=.007$).

As can be seen in Table 1, students in the intervention earned higher course grades than the other two groups ($X2(8)=28.335$, $p<.001$). In the intervention group, the failure rate was 38%. Over half (64%) of the control students received an F. The group as a whole had an average course grade of 0.625. Almost half (45%) of the tutoring group also failed the class. The average course grade was 0.775.

Table 1.
Course Grades

Grade	Intervention	Control	Tutoring
A	1	1	0
B	6	1	1
C	27	12	7
D	6	9	14
F/W	24	41	18

DISCUSSION

Goal Orientation theory suggests that the adoption of mastery goals is accompanied by a host of adaptive academic behaviors and attitudes such as use of effective learning strategies. The intervention described in this paper provided students with knowledge about and practice expressing mastery goals. This should lead the students to begin implementing the adaptive learning strategies.

The intervention produced clear benefits: students in the intervention began to endorse mastery goals to a greater extent and earned higher examination and course grades. These improvements are even more impressive when their performance is compared to that of the control participants and the academic tutoring group.

One could view the control group as a predictor of what could have happened to the intervention group participants without the intervention. These two groups of participants had the same goal orientation profile and the same grades on the first examination. Both sets of students endorsed performance goals more than mastery goals.

After the first examination, the control students' academic work suffered. While other academic behaviors, attitudes, and outcomes were not measured, it could be inferred that these students began to exhibit many of the maladaptive behaviors characteristic of performance oriented students following a challenge. As a result, their grades suffered. The failure rate (D, F) was 78%. Pursuing performance goals while experiencing a challenge did not serve these participants well. These starting conditions would lead one to an equally bleak prediction for the participants in the intervention group.

In contrast, the intervention was able to help students begin to adopt mastery goals. Mastery goal orientation scores increased. This increase was followed by a 9 point increase in examination grades. However, these students scored 12 points on average higher than the control participants. It might be more appropriate to consider this the measure of improvement; over one letter grade. It could be inferred that the adoption of mastery goals enabled these students to begin practicing many of the adaptive academic responses characteristic of mastery goals. The D/F failure rate was nearly cut in half (to 47%).

Further, comparing these results to the academic tutoring group demonstrates that the results are not simply the effect of additional help or contact.   The academic tutoring provided this function. While academic tutoring led to increases in examination grades on the test immediately following the contact, it did not produce the increase in examination grades on subsequent tests and it did not lead to improved course grades.   This is in clear contrast to the improvements observed in the intervention students.   The D/F failure rate was 80% in the academic tutoring students. It appears that students immediately benefit from the gain in knowledge, but that it does not prepare them to handle future challenges.

It is interesting to note that performance goal orientation was not affected by the intervention. None of the techniques used in the intervention group were designed to affect performance goals. Goal orientation theory suggests that mastery and performance goals are orthogonally related (Ames, 1992; Blumenfeld, 1992; Dweck & Leggett, 1988) . These data are consistent with this prediction.

CONCLUSIONS

Overall, the results are quite consistent with goal orientation theory which predicts that increasing the pursuit of mastery goals will lead to the use of adaptive academic behaviors.   This, in turn, can lead to higher levels of academic success. This effect was observed in the present intervention.   As such, this research joins a small set of efforts to apply goal orientation to enhance learning. For example, Aronson and Fried (1998) attempted to increase the endorsement of mastery goals by encouraging an incremental view of competence in an "at risk" college sample.   Their students responded with a marked improvement in grades and enjoyment.

Finally, the improvements resulting from the alteration of goals may have some distinct advantages over other academic interventions. The primary advantage was observed in this study.   Both the goal orientation manipulation and the academic tutoring led to improved test grades.   However, only the intervention produced benefits that continued to accrue after the procedure ended. Thus, goal orientation manipulations offer the potential for transferability across tests, across classes, and over time. In contrast, academic tutoring's benefits are specific to the class and time.   That being said, academic tutoring did produce a valuable increase in academic success. *Perhaps combining goal orientation manipulations with academic tutoring could lead to even bigger improvements and could be considered in future permutations.*

REFERENCES

Albaili, M. (1998). Goal orientation, cognitive strategies and academic achievement among United Arab Emirates college students. *Educational Psychology, 18*, 195-203.

Ames, C. (1992). Classrooms: Goals, structures, and student motivation. *Journal of Educational Psychology, 84*, 261-271.

Ames, C., & Archer, J. (1988). Achievement goals in the classroom: Students' learning strategies and motivation processes. *Journal of Educational Psychology, 80*, 260-267.

Aronson, J., & Fried, C. (1998). *Reducing stereotype threat and boosting academic achievement of African Americans: The role of conceptions of intelligence.* Unpublished manuscript.

Beck, H. P., Rorer-Woody, S., & Pierce, L. G. (1991). The relations of learning and grade orientations to academic performance. *Teaching of Psychology, 15*, 35-37.

Blumenfeld, P.C. (1992). Classroom learning and motivation: Clarifying and expanding goal theory. *Journal of Educational Psychology, 84*, 272-281.

Bouffard, T., Boisvert, J., Vezeau, C., & Larouche, C. (1995). The impact of goal orientation on self-regulation and performance among college students. *British Journal of Educational Psychology, 65*, 317-329.

Dweck, C. S. (1999). *Self-theories: Their role in motivation, personality, and development.* Philadelphia: Psychology Press.

Dweck, C. S. & Leggett, E. L. (1988). A social-cognitive approach to motivation and personality. *Psychological Review, 95*, 256-273.

Elliot, A. J., & Church, M. A. (1997). A hierarchical model of approach and avoidance achievement motivation. *Journal of Personality and Social Psychology, 72*, 218-232.

Elliott, A. J., & Harackiewicz, J. M. (1994). Goal setting, achievement orientation, and intrinsic motivation: A mediational analysis. *Journal of Personality and Social Psychology, 66,* 968-980.

Eppler, M. A. & Harju, B. L. (1997). Achievement motivation goals in relation to academic performance in traditional and non-traditional college students. *Research in Higher Education, 38,* 557-573.

Graham, S., & Golan, S. (1991). Motivational influences on cognition: Task involvement, ego involvement, and depth of information processing. *Journal of Educational Psychology, 83,* 187-194.

Greene, B. A., & Miller, R. B. (1996). Influence on achievement: Goals, perceived ability, and cognitive engagement. *Contemporary Educational Psychology, 21,* 181-192.

Harackiewicz, J. M., Barron, K. E., Carter, S. M., Lehto, A. T., & Elliot, A. J. (1997). Predictors and consequences of achievement goals in the college classroom: Maintaining interest and making the grade. *Journal of Personality and Social Psychology, 73,* 1284-1295.

Harackiewicz, J. M., Barron, K. E., & Elliot, A. J. (1998). Rethinking achievement goals: When are they adaptive for college students and why? *Educational Psychologist, 33,* 1-21.

Harackiewicz, J. M., Barron, K. E., Tauer, J. B., Carter, R. A., & Elliot, A. J. (2000). Short-term and long-term consequences of achievement goals: Predicting interest and performance over time. *Journal of Educational Psychology, 75,* 183-205.

Harackiewicz, J. M., & Elliot, A. J. (1993). Achievement goals and intrinsic motivation. *Journal of Personality and Social Psychology, 65,* 904-915.

Harackiewicz, J. M., & Elliot, A. J. (1998). The joint effects of target and purpose goals on intrinsic motivation: A mediational analysis. *Personality and Social Psychology Bulletin, 24,* 675-689.

Harju, B. L. & Eppler, M. A. (1997). Achievement motivation, flow and irrational beliefs in traditional and nontraditional college students. *Journal of Instructional Psychology, 24,* 147-157.

Hidi, S. & Harackiewicz, J.M. (2000). Motivating the academically unmotivated: A critical issue for the 21st Century. *Review of Educational Research, 70,* 151-179.

Hoyert, M. S. & O'Dell, C. D. (1999, April). *Achievement motivation in traditional and non-traditional students.* Poster presented at the Annual Meeting of the Midwestern Psychological Association, Chicago.

Hoyert, M. S. & O'Dell, C. D. (2000, May). *Achievement motivation and the impostor phenomenon.* Poster presented at the Annual meeting of the Midwestern Psychological Association, Chicago.

Hoyert, M. S. & O'Dell, C. D. (2001, April). *Goal orientation and challenge in college students.* Paper presented at a symposium entitled: Toward a scholarship of teaching and learning in developmental psychology at the Biennial Meeting of the Society for Research in Child Development, Minneapolis.

Hoyert, M. S. & O'Dell, C. D. (2001, May). *Achievement motivation and excuse making.* Poster presented at the Annual meeting of the Midwestern Psychological Association, Chicago.

Hoyert, M. S., & O'Dell, C. D. (In press). The impostor phenomenon and goal orientation. *Journal of the Indiana Academy of Social Sciences.*

Kong, C. & Hau, K. (1996). Student achievement goals and approaches to learning: The relationship between emphasis on self-improvement and thorough understanding. *Research in Education, 55,* 74-85.

Midgley, C. (1993). Motivation and middle level schools. *Advances in Motivation and Achievement, 8,* 217-274.

O'Dell, C. D., & Hoyert, M. S. (2000, April). *Achievement motivation and academic success in traditional and non-traditional aged college students.* Poster presented at the 16th Biennial Meeting of the Conference on Human Development, Memphis, TN.

O'Dell, C. D., & Hoyert, M. S. (2002, May). *Altering achievement motivation and the response to failure.* Poster presented at the CTUP Creative Classroom Poster Session held during the Annual Meeting of the Midwestern Psychological Association, Chicago.
Pintrich, P. R., & Garcia, M. (1991). Student goal orientation and self-regulation in the college classroom. *Advances in Motivation and Achievement, 11,* 123-158.

Pintrich, P. R., & Garcia, M. (1993). Intraindividual differences in students' motivation and self-regulated learning. *German Journal of Educational Psychology, 7,* 99-107.

Pintrich, P. R., & Schunk, D. H. (1996). *Motivation in education: Theory, research, and applications.* Englewood Cliffs, NJ: Prentice Hall.

Pintrich, P. R., Zusho, A., Schiefele, U. & Pekrun, R. (2001). Goal orientation and self-regulated learning in the college classroom: A cross-cultural comparison. In F. Salili, C. Y. Chiu & Y. Y. Hong (Eds.), *Student motivation: The culture and context of learning.* New York: Plenum.

Roedel, T. D. & Schraw, G. (1995). Beliefs about intelligence and academic goals. *Contemporary Educational Psychology, 20,* 464-468.

Roedel, T. D., Schraw, G., & Plake, B. S. (1994). Validation of a measure of learning and performance goal orientations. *Educational and Psychological Measurement, 54,* 1013-1021.

Ryan, A. M., Gheen, H. H., & Midgley, C. (1998). Why do some students avoid asking for help? An examination of the interplay among students' academic efficacy, teachers' social-emotional role, and the classroom goal structure. *Journal of Educational Psychology, 90,* 528-535.

Schraw, G., Horn, C., Thorndike-Christ, T., & Bruning, R. (1995). Academic goal orientations and student classroom achievement. *Contemporary Educational Psychology, 20,* 359-368.

Somuncuoglu, Y. & Yildirim, A. (1999). Relationship between achievement goal orientations and use of learning strategies. *Journal of Educational Research, 92,* 267-277.

Urdan, T. C. (1997). Examining the relations among early adolescent students' goals and friends' orientation toward effort and achievement in school. *Contemporary Educational Psychology, 22,* 165-191.

Urdan, T. C., Kneisel, L., & Mason, V. (1999). Interpreting messages about motivation in the classroom: Examining the effects of achievement goal structures. *Advances in Motivation and Achievement, 11,* 123-158.

Urdan, T. C., & Maehr, M. L. (1995). Beyond a two goal theory of motivation: A case for social goals. *Review of Educational Research, 65,* 213-243.

Urdan, T., Midgley, C., & Anderman, E. (1998). The role of classroom goal structure in students' use of self-handicapping strategies. *American Educational Research Journal, 35,* 101-122.

Wolters, C. A., Yu, S. L., & Pintrich, P. R. (1996). The relation between goal orientation and students' motivational beliefs and self-regulated learning. *Learning and Individual Differences, 8,* 211-238.

PROMOTING CRITICAL THINKING SKILLS

THROUGH REFLECTION PAPERS

AND THE INTERNET

Wendy L. Jordanov
Tennessee State University

INTRODUCTION

Encouraging students to think deeply about subjects encountered in lectures, class discussions, and in textbooks is a task many college professors struggle to achieve. Educational research suggests that students learn better when they are engaged in their learning rather than passive recipients of information (Kolb, 1984). College classes around the country are employing the use of technological tools such as on-line discussion rooms, chat rooms, and class Websites to help engage students in critical thinking. Is this an effective way of encouraging students to think more deeply and consider multiple perspectives about subjects, topics, opinions, and theories? What do college students think about these technological tools? This paper reports the results of a qualitative survey of college student attitudes regarding reflection papers and the Internet.

BACKGROUND INFORMATION

Pascarella (1999) compared changes in critical thinking over a one-year period between matched groups of college and non-college students. Results indicate that students who attended college for one year scored higher in critical thinking than the matched group of students who did not attend. Possible reasons for this difference could be related to environmental influences, peer support, course activities and assignments. Finkel (1999) used class discussions, writing of position papers, and exposure to opposite viewpoints to encourage deeper thinking among students in two psychology classes. Quantitative and qualitative data from student evaluations suggested that the discussions improved interaction, engaged students in the issues, and promoted critical thinking.

Constructivist theory is the basis for a variety of technology-based active and collaborative learning assignments. Constructivism emphasizes the active building of knowledge by encouraging the learner to be an active meaning maker and to solve problems (Glatthorn, 1994). College-level writing assignments on student reactions and opinions encourage more reading of assignments, broader student participation, higher levels of discussion, and a more positive student experience (Valde, 1997).

The use of on-line discussion rooms is an alternative to the traditional writing assignment. In contrast to turning in a paper for the teacher to read, on-line discussions allow everyone in the class to read each other's papers. Due to the fact that classroom time is limited, students often hear only the responses of a select few volunteers. The use of on-line discussion rooms allows all students to respond to questions and issues, thus giving them a chance to formulate their own perspective on a topic.

Pascarella et al., (2001) found that students' involvement in diversity experiences during college had statistically significant positive effects on their scores on an objective, standardized measure of critical thinking skills. Opportunities for students to explore the diverse viewpoints and ideas of their peers lend themselves well to generating excitement, engaging students, and promoting ownership of problems in a supportive environment. Technology-enhanced learning environments can encourage interaction among students and faculty and allow for flexibility in student time for engaging in learning.

THE STUDY

Undergraduate students in human development courses were asked to participate in a semester-long study. A variety of debatable topics were addressed in the text and classroom lectures. Some students shared their viewpoints with classmates in class-wide discussions. Due to the time constraints of the courses, many students did not have ample opportunity to share their thoughts or perspectives.

An alternative to in-class discussions on these topics was used. Students were asked to write reflection papers on specific topics from class. These papers were posted on a class Website and students were required to review the papers of at least two peers. During the course of the semester, students wrote a total of four reflection papers. The topics used to encourage multiple perspectives were nature versus nurture, gender roles, creativity and moral development.

At the end of the semester, students were asked to evaluate the value of the reflection papers. Fifty-eight students were enrolled in these classes and at the end of the semester fifty students agreed to participate in this study. Participants were asked to complete one Likert-type question and two open-ended questions. The Likert-type question asked: *Did participating in these technology-based perspective-taking assignments help you to think more clearly and critically about the nature versus nurture debate, gender roles, creativity and moral development?* One open-ended question asked: *What were the benefits and/or hindrances of participating in these perspective-*

taking assignments?   The second open-ended question asked for additional comments about these assignments.

FINDINGS

Results of the survey of student perceptions of posted reflection papers indicated that a majority of students valued these assignments. Forty-seven students agreed that participating in these assignments helped them to think more clearly and critically about the nature versus nurture debate, gender roles, creativity and moral development. Three students were neutral.

For the open-ended questions, 38 students shared positive comments, 10 did not comment and 2 wrote that they would rather turn in their papers to the professor. Several students reported that they found these assignments To be either eye-opening, thought-provoking, or challenging. Students shared that they:

Enjoyed exploring [their] classmates' opinions and views on various topics

Thought about gender roles in a different light after reading what others wrote

Learned that people can be creative even if they are not artistic

A few students commented on the value of being exposed to perspectives different from their own in order to better understand a topic or issue. One student wrote:

I did not really understand Kohlberg's level 5 until I read some of my classmates' papers.

Another student explained:

> *I always thought my intelligence was fixed based on my genetics. Now, I see that my environment can affect my intelligence to some degree.*

Some students reported that these assignments improved learning and encouraged critical thinking about topics covered in class. Students commented:

> *I learned a lot of information from reading my peers' papers*

> *Reading these papers caused me to really think about topics I had taken for granted*

Students also shared that they enjoyed these assignments and put more effort into these assignments than they would have for traditional papers on the same topics.

> *I enjoyed writing these papers because I wanted to share my views with others*

Students reported that they worked harder on their papers because they knew their classmates would be able to read them.

> *I worked twice as hard on this paper because I knew my friends would be reading it*

Students also noticed that they were more willing and able to understand alternative perspectives on issues after completing these assignments. Student stated:

When I wrote my paper, I thought my answer was the RIGHT answer. After reading some of the others' papers, I see that there is more than one right answer

At first, I didn't want my friends reading my paper, but it ended up being fun and interesting

CONCLUSIONS

Critical thinking skills are valuable tools sought by many college students today. By using reflection papers on the Internet, teachers can assist students in the development of critical thinking skills. The unique factor of these assignments is that they are not simply printed out and handed in to the professor. Instead, these assignments are posted on the class Website for all students to access. Once all of the papers are written, students are asked to read each other's papers and write responses that are also posted for everyone to access. This process of communicating with each other encourages students to explore viewpoints that may be very different from their own. Reflection papers offer students a chance to interact with each other and explore the course material in a deeper way.

REFERENCES

Finkel, D. (1999).   Enhancing student involvement and comprehension through group and class discussions. *Journal on Excellence in College Teaching, 10*(3), 33-48.

Glatthorn A. A. (1994). Constructivism: implications for curriculum. *International Journal of Educational Reform, 3* (4), 449-55.

Kolb, D. (1984). *Experiential learning: Experience as the source of learning and development.*   Englewood Cliffs, NJ: Prentice-Hall.

Pascarella, E. T. (1999). The development of critical thinking: Does college make a difference? *Journal of College Student Development, 40*(5), 562-69.

Pascarella, E. T., Palmer, B., Moye, M., & Pierson, C. T. (2001). Do diversity experiences influence the development of critical thinking? *Journal of College Student Development, 42*(3), 257-71.

Valde, Gregory A. (1997). Promoting student participation and learning through the use of weekly writing assignments. *Journal on Excellence in College Teaching, 8* (3), 67-76.

JUST DON'T MAKE ME THINK:

METACOGNITION IN COLLEGE CLASSES

Kathleen King
Idaho State University

INTRODUCTION

At the beginning of October, I held one-on-one conferences with my students. These one-on-one meetings turned out as usual: some students were eager to work with me on the outline for their next paper, others were anxious about meeting with a professor, and a smaller third group – those who believe homework is optional—hadn't completed the required assignment. Many college students don't know how to write and don't want to improve their skills. This is rooted in a fear of the new coupled with a distaste for learning. During her conference, one student put her hand to her forehead and said, "Just don't make me think. I hate it when we have to think. It gives me a headache."

If college teachers can engage students in learning how to solve academic problems, these learners will be able to use both cognition and metacognition to good effect, not only in higher education, but also in real life. College teachers can use metacognition to help students develop the ability to analyze and adapt their thinking, learning, and writing processes. Drawing on personal observation and a survey of published literature, this paper explores the history and definition of the term metacognition, discusses how to distinguish between cognition and metacognition, describes methods for assessing students' metacognitive skills, investigates how to build metacognitive experiences into courses, and recommends that teachers also practice metacognitive thinking.

DEFINITION AND HISTORY OF THE TERM "METACOGNITION"

Metacognition became a buzzword in education during the mid-1970s, especially for teachers of reading and special education. Metacognition can be defined as "thinking about thinking." It is important to be clear and precise about this complex form of higher-order thought. Metacognition involves not only the ability to think about one's own thinking, but also includes knowing how to analyze thought, how to draw conclusions from the analysis, and how to put into practice what has been learned. In fostering metacognition, teachers encourage students to become aware of and understand how they and others think.

Metacognitive theory draws on the work of Plato, Aristotle, Confucius, Lao Tzu, Solomon, and Buddha, great thinkers who understood the importance of insight in learning. In 1690, John Locke observed that most children gradually develop the ability to reflect on their own thinking processes, although some children never do.

Strategies for assessing and teaching metacognitive skills were in use long before the term became popular. Reading was an early focus of research on reflective thinking. In 1909, Baldwin used a questionnaire to learn how students' read, and a year later Dewey introduced "reflective reading." For Dewey, reflection was a special kind of thinking involving the ordering and linking of ideas. By 1917, Thorndike was asking students to problem-solve by answering questions on texts they had read (Brown 1987; Hatton & Smith 1995). In 1963, Flavell (1963) published "The Developmental Psychology of Jean Piaget," and planning as a distinct form of higher order thinking once again caught the interest of researchers. In 1971, Flavell introduced the term "metamemory" and conducted the first study of children's metamemory (Flavell, 1971). By 1975, the word "metacognition" had come into common use.

DISTINGUISHING BETWEEN COGNITION AND METACOGNITION

Hacker (1998) mentions that Kluwe refined the concept of metacognition by noting two characteristics: the thinker knows something about his or her own and others' thought processes, and the thinker can pay attention to and change his or her thinking. Kluwe calls this second type of metacognition "executive processes." Pointing out the difference between cognitive tasks (remembering things learned earlier that might help with the current task or problem) and metacognitive tasks (monitoring and directing the process of problem solving), Hacker stresses the importance of learning more about thinking. An additional point is made by Cornoldi (1998), who emphasizes the role of learners' beliefs about thinking. If students feel confident that they can solve problems, they do better work.

In 1987, Weinert (1987) wrote about the apparent ease of separating the two types of thinking, defining metacognition as simply "thinking about thinking" or "second-order cognition" (p. 8). However, he acknowledges that purpose, conscious understanding, ability to talk or write about tasks, and generalizability to other tasks are important factors in determining whether or not a given task is metacognitive. Brown (1987) agrees that metacognition requires the thinker to use and describe the process of mental activity. Allen and Armour-Thomas (1991) both include knowledge about and control over thinking processes in defining metacognition, while

Vadhan and Stander (1993) clearly separate ordinary thinking from awareness and understanding of thinking. Hacker (1998) divides metacognitive thinking into three types:

- Metacognitive knowledge (what one knows about knowing)

- Metacognitive skill (what one is currently doing)

- Metacognitive experience (one's current cognitive or affective state)

While *cognition* focuses on *solving* the problem, *metacognition* focuses on the *process* of solving the problem. According to Marchant (2001), "Metacognitive skills involve knowing what to do, and how and when to do it" (p. 488). In college classes, students have the opportunity to learn how to plan their thinking and learning, and in doing so, they acquire skills which enable them to engage in more effective decision-making throughout their lives.

FACTORS WHICH AFFECT METACOGNITION

Although much of what we know about metacognition grew out of the work of specialists in reading and learning disabilities, this information also can be applied to many types of college classes. Flavell (1987) points out the importance of knowing how three variables interact.

Person Variables. These involve the learner's beliefs about how he or she and others think and learn. For instance, a student who believes that she is mathematically challenged may not do well in math classes simply because she lacks the confidence necessary to do the work.

Task Variables. These include how difficult a problem is and how that affects the process the learner uses. Some students tend to simply give up when faced with a difficult or unfamiliar problem.

Strategy Variables. These are also important. Cognitive strategy may involve knowing how to do a particular task, but higher-order metacognitive strategy includes checking to see that the solution to the problem is correct and that the goal has been reached. Learners need metacognitive skills often, especially in new situations, where correctness is important, and when difficulty develops.

Executive Decisions

Going a step further, Kluwe (1987) separates executive decisions from other types of metacognition. Executive decisions focus on *how* to solve a problem rather than just getting the answer, develop from the need to avoid failure, and may not be needed when completing some tasks. Brown (1987) points out that one weakness of executive decision theory is its source in theories of synthetic (artificial, computer) intelligence. Although marvelous thinking machines have been developed, for instance, IBM's Deep Blue, which beat world champion Garry Kasparov at chess (Deep Blue Wins Match, 2002), synthetic intelligence differs from human intelligence in important ways. For an interesting experience with synthetic intelligence, read about and talk with Richard Wallace's chatbot A.L.I.C.E. at www.alicebot.com . Some of this author's students believe that A.L.I.C.E. is a near-miracle, while others soon conclude that the chatbot's weaknesses include saying the same thing over and over and a limited fund of knowledge.

ASSESSING METACOGNITIVE SKILLS

Writing teachers look for certain skills in their students.   The table below combines descriptions of characteristics supplied by Collins (1994), Sitko (1998), Gourgey (1999), Paris and Paris (2001), with observations by this author.   It is easy to spot writers who may have trouble by comparing this list of behaviors with the skills of individual students.

Table 1
Differences Between Skilled
and Less-Experienced Writers

Skilled writers	Less experienced writers
Write more	Write less
Active	Passive
Feel confident of skills	Insecure, worried about skills
Have repertoire of strategies	Have few strategies
Ask questions, take notes	Overlook important ideas because
Consider rhetorical goals such as	they do not engage in self-
purpose, audience, genre	questioning and self-testing
Understand conventions of genre	Forget to consider purpose and
Figure things out for themselves	audience
	Lack knowledge of genre
	Rely on others for clarification
	May have mistaken notions of
	how writers work
	Frustrated, give up easily
	Daydream, forget assignments
Divide process into parts	Tend to organize ideas by using a
Use subgoals as motivation	list
Allocate time and resources	Don't use memory or
judiciously	environment to generate content
Relate information to previous	Don't understand how to manage
knowledge	a task
	Fail to relate the present task to
	previous knowledge

Better at revision Can detect, diagnose, and fix problems in their own texts and those of others	Often decide to leave problems in the text untouched Seek help with sentence-level errors from older people
Complete assignments in a timely manner Talk to professor, arrange conferences	Complete assignments at the last minute May fail to finish or hand in assignments Avoid professor, fail to show up for conferences

This author has used the above list of strategies in several ways. If the list of strategies is handed out to students on the first day of class, they can be asked to check off their usual methods of completing assignments. A student can then review her/his progress in using metacognition at several points during the semester by writing letters to the professor which discuss how problem solving techniques were used in specific assignments.

Another way to use the list of strategies is to focus a final examination question on what students have learned about metacognition. Students bring all their work for the semester to the examination and write an essay which describes what they learned about thinking, using examples from their graded work to prove their main points.

A simple test of whether or not students possess metacognitive thinking is "The Frog Puzzle" (1975), which this author received as a handout from the Nebraska Writing Project in the summer of 1982. The puzzle tells the story of a professor who caught, banded, and released frogs in a pond, and then on a second trip, caught a number of frogs and counted how many had bands. Using the information given, students are asked to complete two tasks: 1) compute the total number of frogs in the pond; and 2) write down the method they used to come up with the answer. Answers fall into three categories. The first type of student thinks concretely and writes that the problem cannot be solved with the available data. The second type of student, on the verge of making the breakthrough into abstract thinking, gets the number of frogs wrong but understands that there is some method which can be used to calculate the total number of frogs in the pond. The third type of student, able to easily move from the data provided to the abstract thought required to construct the equation that solves the puzzle, comes up with the correct answer and has no trouble explaining how it was done.   This simple problem reveals which students are able to engage in metacognition and which students need help to make a breakthrough.

Another instrument for measuring higher-order thinking is the "Components of Metacognition Questionnaire" adapted by this author from the work of Allen and Armour-Thomas (1991). This questionnaire asks people to rate themselves using a five-point scale on a series of tasks that may be approached cognitively or metacognitively. Each section focuses on one aspect of metacognition, including defining the nature of a problem, options for problem-solving, using strategy, selecting a representation for information (mental mapping), allocating resources, and evaluating how well a solution worked. Students with higher scores are more likely to possess a higher level of metacognitive skill.

The "Vividness of Visual Imagery Questionnaire" developed by Marks (1999) takes a different approach, equating metacognition with the ability to "form mental pictures, or to 'see in the mind's eye'" (p. 11). Marks argues that, "Mental practice which employs subjectively experienced images of future events—and explores how these events might be influenced by behavioral intervention—enables the experiencer's future actions towards her/his goals." (p. 2).

The questionnaire asks students to visualize four different images, first with eyes open and then with eyes closed, and rate them on a five–point scale (the ratings were inverted by this author for consistency with other questionnaires, so that a higher score indicates a greater ability to form mental images). The five points ranged from "clear and vivid as normal vision"—worth 5 points; to "no image at all"—valued at 1 (p. 11). Marks concludes that the ability to form mental images is an important part of goal directed thinking and action. Forming a mental image of the path to be followed is one step in the process of solving a problem or completing a task.

The "Holistic Critical Thinking Scoring Rubric" developed by Facione and Facione (1994) can help teachers evaluate students' performance in critical thinking, a skill which in their definition seems similar to metacognition. Because these writers define critical thinking as the ability to understand an assignment, focus on relevant rather than irrelevant information, store information, and try out new strategies, this scoring system may give a teacher some insight into metacognitive ability.

Graham and Wong (1993) developed a questionnaire for assessing metacognition in readers that this author adapted for writers as the "Metacognitive Writing Skills Questionnaire." This simple questionnaire asks students to describe their feelings about writing and experiences with it, looking for strengths, weaknesses, and what needs to be learned in the future.

Another quick way to estimate metacognitive ability is suggested by Vadhan and Stander (1993). They asked students to estimate what grade they would receive. The actual grade in the course measures cognitive ability, but looking at how close the student's estimate came to the final grade measures metacognition. Students who lack this ability may honestly believe that they are doing well in a class and often feel crushed when they receive low grades.

METACOGNITION
AND LEARNING HOW TO WRITE

   The writing process can be organized in many ways. Ask students to draw a picture or diagram of the steps they go through when writing a paper. You will learn a great deal about how they perceive the writing process. A beginning freshman composition student may create a straight-forward diagram much like this:

Look up some stuff on the Web

Write the paper

Get my Mom to look at it.

An English professor might draw a diagram more like Figure 1 below.

Figure 1
The Author's Writing Process

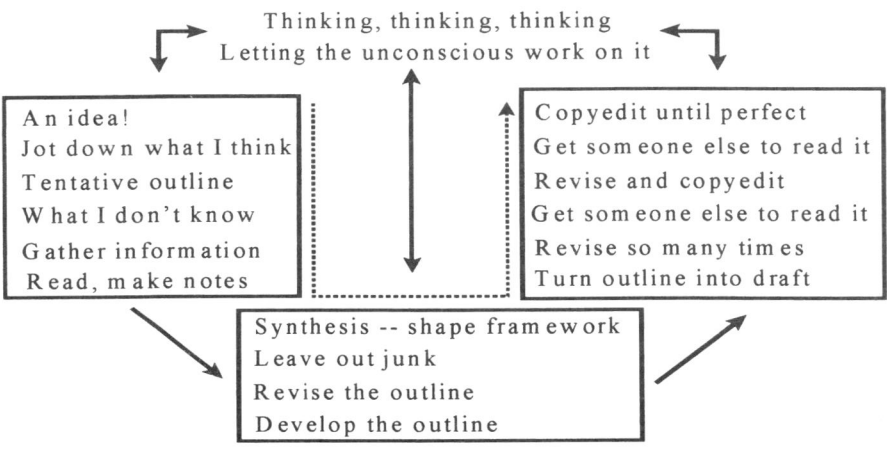

Figure 1 emphasizes the reflexive nature of the writing process, with each stage of writing moving back and forth between conscious thought, using the unconscious, and actual work on the project. The process moves from the initial idea and information gathering stage, to synthesis and outlining, and finally through drafting, multiple revisions, advice from a critical reader, and copyediting. The fourteen-part process can be simplified by organizing it into task blocks. Another list might shape the writing process into four steps:

- Planning

- Drafting

- Revising

- Copyediting

Experienced writers find it easy to construct a sequence, but those who are fearful or simply haven't done enough writing to know how the process works may need help in learning how to construct a strategy for attacking a writing task. Another possibility is that inexperienced writing students simply haven't been taught to think of writing as a process which can be analyzed and learned. Such students lack knowledge about how writers work and consistently subscribe to the myth of the perfect first draft—that good writers sit down at the computer and produce a perfect document in about an hour. Of course, teachers and more experienced writers know how false this notion is, but it's a difficult misconception to overcome.

Sitko (1998) recommends that teachers develop " . . . explicit guides to reduce the strain on working memory by encouraging a range of activities such as goal setting and problem identification . . . facilitations in the form of cards, verbal cues, or computer-generated prompts" (p. 102). Prompts designed to elicit metacognition can be used at any stage in the process, and college students may need help at many stages, including coming up with ideas, setting goals and planning how to reach those goals, synthesizing research materials, drafting, global revision, sentence-level revision, and careful copyediting. Sitko notes that students who received instruction in global and rhetorical revision strategies were able to improve their writing more than those who did not receive such instruction, which indicates that metacognitive strategies can be taught and learned.

When planning a specific writing lesson that will also teach metacognition, teachers can follow guidelines created by Paris and Paris (2001) and Bereiter and Scadamalia (Sitko, 1998). Writing about self-regulated learning, a classroom technique which uses metacognition, Paris and Paris suggest that tasks which help students develop higher order thinking should be interesting, collaborative, difficult rather than easy, with opportunities for success. Choose a specific task that novices don't do—based on your assessment of the metacognitive skills of students—and develop an explicit description of the mental operations involved in the task. Create a plan to let students know how and when to begin and end the process, and then develop cards, mnemonics, and routines to help students remember what to do (Sitko, 1998).

It is not enough to teach just the strategies. Teachers must also demonstrate how, when, and why to use each strategy. Coaching and in-class practice enable students to try out techniques in a safe environment and in peer groups. Students should recognize the cause-and-effect results of applying strategies and becoming better writers.

For instance, Gourgey (1999) designed two exercises to help students develop metacognitive skills. The first assignment, "Vocabulary in Context," asks students to analyze Lewis Carroll's "Jabberwocky," which "is composed largely of nonsense words, yet . . . tells an understandable story" (p. 2). Working collaboratively in small groups, the students read the poem and figure out definitions for as many words as possible. Beyond the surface exercise, students are asked to think metacognitively by focusing attention on the process they use to solve the problem of words that seem to have no meaning.

Gourgey's second exercise focuses on "Metacognitive Reading Strategies." Students presented with a newspaper article must generate questions and predictions about the article. Then students read the article, find answers to their questions, see how accurate their predictions are, generate new questions and answer them, and note when they feel confused and how they resolve this feeling. The students then report their experiences with the task. After a review of how to write summaries, they decide what to include in their own summaries of articles. The students are enthusiastic about the exercise, but Gourgey notes that, "When I repeated this procedure using progressively lengthier and more technical passages, students still struggled to master the metacognitive skills, and needed to review them again and again . . . only by struggling with these skills over time did they begin to develop the confidence that they could figure out meaning for themselves" (p. 6).

Writing experts Elbow and Belanoff (2000) divide revision into three stages or levels: changing the bones, changing the muscles, and copyediting. An exercise on changing the muscles—a type of global revision—asks students to print drafts of their papers with three inch right margins. In the first part of the exercise, each writer creates a paragraph " . . . which states briefly your purpose for writing the paper and the reasons why you chose to accomplish your purpose in the way you did" (p. 157).

Then each writer goes through the draft paper paragraph by paragraph and writes in the wide margin, "a summary of what the paragraph says and does (its purpose), and how it fits in where it is." Afterward, group members write margin notes on each other's papers and jot down their emotional responses to each paragraph. Using the information generated by this exercise, the writers can then restructure, rewrite, or add to their papers.

Peer group analysis and discussion is particularly useful. Students have fun sharing their work, but also— most importantly—they see how others in the class take on and accomplish tasks, thus enabling them to generalize about strategies as well as learning and trying out specific techniques. Peer groups enable students to work together as they learn how to analyze the requirements of a task, make a new plan for completing an assignment, proceed through steps toward a goal, figure out how well the strategies worked, and make a plan to work more effectively next time.

The strategies learned in a writing course can also be applied to other opportunities to learn, think, manage work, and solve problems. Of course, metacognition should always be practiced within actual assignments, not in isolation (Paris & Paris, 2001). Overall strategies should be planned to focus on the separate parts of a project, perhaps by requiring that research materials, an outline, or a draft paper be brought to class to share in peer groups. This allows students to learn from their mistakes and successes, adjusting their plans as the project proceeds. Throughout an assignment, students should have opportunities for self- and teacher-assessment to make sure they are on the right track and to help them correct problems.

USING METACOGNITION
TO ASSESS PERFORMANCE

One valuable method of grading involves both student and teacher: portfolio-based assessment. Although this form of grading has been used most commonly in writing classes, other fields also lend themselves to portfolio use. Students, perhaps during conferences with the teacher, go through their work and select examples that show the progress they have made. A letter or essay accompanying the portfolio discusses what the student found difficult, which samples show his or her best work, how the examples demonstrate progress, his or her feelings about the work and how those feelings may have changed, and how he or she responded to periodic evaluations by the teacher (Paris & Paris, 2001). In addition, students should be asked to assess what they learned from didactic instruction, how they practiced using thinking strategies, what they didn't understand, and what they still need to learn.

Murray (1990) describes how commentaries on writing teach both students and instructor. He and his students wrote about their writing and shared these documents. Both teacher and students found that this exercise helped define what they did well and made it easier to find solutions to problems. The tone for these letters is " ...that of a letter to a friend who is also writing" (p. 20). Murray asks students to focus on the emotions they feel when writing, the techniques they use when writing goes well, how problems are solved, the connections between reading and writing, and the overall process they use. He notes that this type of writing enables writers to learn from themselves and each other.

Elbow and Belanoff (2000) point out that metacognition gives students power and control over their learning and writing. Improving as a writer means looking at what, how, and why people write the way they do. These authors describe Vygotsky's conclusion that higher learning depends on what you already know.   Today's college students tend to not know much about writing.   If students have trouble writing, they need to know how to analyze the problem to figure out what works and what doesn't work.

Marchant (2001) suggests a more direct approach to metacognition.   She points to Woolfolk's recommendation that students be actively taught strategies, when to use them, and what the positive effects of using writing strategies will be.   In other words, we need to teach students metacognitive skills and build in opportunities to practice and refine what they have learned.

One way to get college students thinking metacognitively is demonstrated by Giancarlo and Facione's (2002) one page "The Reflective Log" handout for a senior capstone course in liberal studies.   They stress that metacognition is a skill exhibited by good thinkers, whether or not these people are highly educated.   The assignment asks students to keep a log for nine weeks. Students make daily entries in their logbooks, writing about and perhaps diagramming their thoughts.   At the end of each week, students write a final paragraph that relates an important learning experience and evaluates the quality of thinking they did.   Weekly questions help students gradually develop the ability to "analyze, interpret, explain, and evaluate one's thinking by the standards of good reasoning."

METACOGNITION FOR TEACHERS, TOO

Borkowski (1992) points out that, "Teachers desperately need explicit examples of how to teach children to carry out task analyses, how to scan past experiences for a range of viable strategies, how to match task demands to the strategy set in order to select the best strategy, and how to monitor and revise the initial strategy selection" (p. 256). But where do teachers find such models? One way is to develop working models based on experience and interaction with others.

The use of "critical friend" dyads is recommended by Hatton and Smith (1995). This pattern of reflection with a peer who can be trusted to be honest, questioning, and thoughtful enables teachers to think aloud and explore new ideas which they might not think of when working alone. Such cooperative learning works well with Marchant's (2001) method for the reflective practitioner who wants to create knowledge. In this model, the teacher asks critical questions about how students can learn metacognitive skills, conducts an "experiment"—an exercise which combines knowledge, practice, and self-analysis—to solve the problem, and then learns from how the experiment did and did not succeed, developing a new exercise in the process.

College is difficult for many students. The younger ones may be focused on "the college experience" of hanging out with friends, while thirtyish non-traditional students have jobs, children, and mortgages to worry about. Despite the differing needs of various types of students, all can benefit from learning metacognitive strategies. By actively encouraging metacognition, college teachers give their students the power to optimize thinking and learning, a skill which they will use throughout their lives. If our students can assess problems and develop plans to solve them, check and adjust their behavior so that the results are positive, and evaluate their successes and failures so that they learn what will work next time, they will have a good start on a lifetime of successful thinking—without the headaches.

REFERENCES

Allen, B. A., & Armour-Thomas, E. (1991). Construct validation of metacognition. *Journal of Psychology, 127*(2), 203-211.

Borkowski, J. G. (1992). Metacognitive theory: A framework for teaching literacy, writing, and math skills. *Journal of Learning Disabilities, 25*(4), 253-257.

Brown, A. (1987). Metacognition, executive control, self-regulation, and other more mysterious mechanisms. In F. Weinert, & R. Kluwe (Eds.), *Metacognition, motivation, and understanding* (pp. 65-116). Hillsdale, NJ: Erlbaum.

Collins, N.D. (1994). *Metacognition and reading to learn.* (Report No. EDO-CS-94-9). East Lansing, MI: National Center for Research on Teacher Learning.

Cornoldi, C. (1998). The impact of metacognitive reflection on cognitive control. In G. Mazzoni, & T. Nelson (Eds.), *Metacognition and cognitive neuropsychology* (pp. 139-159). Mahwah, NJ: Erlbaum.

Deep Blue Wins Match. (2002). Retrieved October 21, 2002 from http://www.research.ibm.com/deepblue/home/may11/story_1.html .

Elbow, P., & Belanoff, P. (2000). *A community of writers: A workshop course in writing.* Boston: McGraw Hill.

Facione, P. A., & Facione, N. C. (1994). *Holistic critical thinking scoring rubric.* Retrieved August 22, 2002 from http://www.insightassessment.com/HCTSR.html.

Flavell, J. H. (1963). The developmental psychology of Jean Piaget. New York: Van Nostrand Reinhold.

Flavell, J. H. (1971). First discussant's comments: What is memory development the development of? *Human Development, 14*, 272-278.

Flavell, J. H. (1987). Speculations about the nature and development of metacognition. In F. Weinert & R. Kluwe (Eds.), *Metacognition, motivation, and understanding* (pp. 21-29). Hillsdale, NJ: Erlbaum.

Giancarlo, C. A., & Facione, P. A. (2002). The reflective log. In *Critical thinking as reasoned judgment, the album.* Santa Clara, CA: Insight Assessment and The California Academic Press.

Gourgey, A. F. (1999). Teaching reading from a metacognitive perspective: Theory and classroom experiences. *Journal of College Reading and Learning,* 30(1), 85.

Graham, L., & Wong, B.Y. (1993). Comparing two modes of teaching a question-answering strategy for enhancing reading comprehension: Didactic and self-instructional training. *Journal of Learning Disabilities, 26* (4), 270-279.

Hacker, D. J. (1998). Definitions and empirical foundations. In D. Hacker, J. Dunlosky, & A. Graesser (Eds.), *Metacognition in educational theory and practice* (pp. 1-23). Mahwah, NJ: Erlbaum.

Hatton, N., & Smith, D. (1995). *Reflection in teacher education: Towards definition and implementation.* Retrieved August 22, 2002 from http://alex.edfac.usyd.edu.au/LocalResource/Study1/hattonart.html .

Kluwe, R. H. (1987). Executive decisions and regulation of problem solving behavior. In F. Weinert, & R. Kluwe (Eds.), *Metacognition, motivation, and understanding* (pp. 31-64). Hillsdale, NJ: Erlbaum.

Marchant, G. J. (2001). Metateaching: A metaphor for reflective teaching. *Education, 109*(4), 487-489.

Marks, D.   (1999). Consciousness, mental imagery and action. *British Journal of Psychology, 99*(4), 567+. Retrieved August 22, 2002 from the InfoTrac database.

Murray, D. M. (1990). *Write to learn.* Fort Worth: Holt, Rinehart, and Winston.

Paris, S. G., & Paris, A.H. (2001). Classroom applications of research on self-regulated learning. *Educational Psychologist, 36*(2), 89-101.

Sitko, B. M. (1998). Knowing how to write: Metacognition and writing instruction. In D. Hacker, J. Dunlosky, & A. Graesser (Eds.), *Metacognition in educational theory and practice* (pp. 93-115). Mahwah, NJ: Erlbaum.

The Frog Puzzle. (1975). Berkeley, CA: Regents of the University of California.

Vadhan, V., & Stander, P. (1993). Metacognitive ability and test performance among college students. *Journal of Psychology, 128*(3), 307-309.

Weinert, F. E. (1987). Introduction and overview: Metacognition and motivation as determinants of effective learning and understanding. In F. Weinert & R. Kluwe (Eds.), *Metacognition, motivation, and understanding* (pp. 1-19). Hillsdale, NJ: Erlbaum.

FACULTY PROFESSIONAL DEVELOPMENT:

THEY CAN TEACH BUT WILL THEY LEARN?

Ron Liss
Montgomery College

INTRODUCTION

Professional development for faculty in higher education has been an ongoing practice for a long time. Gaff (1975) identified over 200 faculty development programs in 1975. There are a variety of writings on what constitutes a faculty development program. This often includes how faculty need to accommodate adult learners in classes (Fitzgibbon, 2002) and (Alfano, 1993). How adults learn has been studied extensively as a separate topic. However, only a few authors have approached faculty development in light of faculty as adult learners. This paper is aimed at bringing this issue forward to explain why many faculty do not benefit from professional development offerings, and how the situation can be improved.

Educators come to institutions of higher learning for a variety of reasons. One of their responsibilities is to lead a classroom of students. They may teach or they may help students learn. They may profess, facilitate, lead, guide, or lecture. If you ask a faculty member if this is part of their profession they may give a *resounding* yes or a *meek* yes depending on the emphasis they give to their classroom duties. Clearly, however, faculty are some type of teacher.

Another role faculty understand is that they are constantly developing. The direction this development goes is multidimensional and is categorized in a variety of ways. Generally it is classified into improving teaching, faculty scholarship, personal, curriculum or institutional development (Brawer,1990). Alfano (1993) feels that faculty development provides an economically reasonable way to improve educational outcomes and maintain institutional integrity. The improving teaching aspect of faculty development is categorized as pedagogical professional development. *What does pedagogical professional development incorporate and how can faculty be attracted?*

Faculty are central to this discussion. They change their role and become students or learners in professional development activities. Not only are they learners, but they are adult learners.   Elliot, Skeff, and Stratos (1999) instituted a longitudinal faculty development program for physician educators with a premise that says: "Focusing on improving teaching abilities is similar to other programs designed to alter behavior, such as interventions to deter substance abuse or promote regular exercise" (p. 52).

Manzo (1996) provides several reasons for faculty development centers. They include a renewed focus on learning, technology, student demand for quality education, and accountability. Millis (1994) describes faculty development as including newsletters, discussion groups, individual consultation, workshops and seminars, mentoring, classroom observations, career counseling, research assistance, and sabbaticals. However, beyond Lawler and King's (2000) text, "Planning Effective Faculty Development: Using Adult Learning Strategies," there is little written that urges the use of adult learning principles when designing and delivering pedagogical professional development.

Oromaner (1998) tells us:

Each institution must confront the issue of faculty and staff participation.   Efforts to increase participation range from reliance on internalized professional and career norms and values concerning development to formal requirements written into individual development plans and collective bargaining agreements. Monetary incentives also have proven quite successful (p. 3).

The added premise of delivering professional development in a mode that fits the adult learner needs attention. A series of questions to be answered through a literature review of both adult learning principles and faculty development activities will help put substance to this concept. The questions are composed from the perspective of a faculty member who has decided *not* to participate in pedagogical professional development. The answers use literature as the grounding to address the problem and justify the answer. The answers provide an overview of what the literature tells us about how adults learn, how faculty professional development organizations develop and deliver their programs, and a perspective on the intersection of these two and how that effects faculty participation in professional development programs.

BACKGROUND INFORMATION

I can't go to that presentation. Why are staff going to be there?

This speaks to the need for adult learners to be in a non-threatening learning environment. Faculty development programs and centers serve various purposes for higher education institutions. Faculty development is often coordinated by faculty committees or by campus-wide teaching, media or research centers (Millis, 1994). Depending on the focus of the coordinating group faculty programs may not be restricted to only faculty. *Why*? One reason is that this may be financially and logistically advantageous to the institution.

A comprehensive Website has been developed by Honolulu Community College (2003) as part of their faculty development program. There is a variety of information available that is not credited to an individual or group but is a valuable resource for all educators. It received a 2003 National Council for Staff, Program and Organizational Development (NCSPOD) Innovation Award. The page titled "Principles of Adult Learning" (Honolulu Community College, 2003) provides guidance in treating learners as adults.

One of the concepts advocated in the above is that adults have pride, which must be considered as a factor in faculty development. Faculty participating in professional development are there to learn new concepts or skills. Their ego may not accept that the staff be exposed to their weaknesses.

Cross (1981) ranks different types of learning opportunities with their level of risk or threat. The least risk begins with self-directed and moves up the risk scale with televised courses as unregistered learners, noncredit adult education, competency-based learning, and credit classes. While professional development does not fit perfectly into any of these categories, it is in the higher threat arena. Recognizing and accommodating the threats perceived by faculty must be addressed.

I can teach this stuff. Why didn't they ask me? or What can they teach me?

These are reasonable questions. Colleges often use external consultants to deliver workshops, research a topic and deliver it using professional development personnel, or use faculty associated with a professional development center.

Another concept from the "Principles of Adult Learning" (Honolulu Community College, 2003) is that adults are people with years of experience and a wealth of information. Lawler and King tell us "We can rely on a wealth of information regarding adult learners, including their own experiences" (2000, p. 43). Faculty can help in the development and subsequent delivery of many topics. This provides benefit to the institution and caters to the faculty as an adult learner. Faculty often consult with other institutions and present papers at conferences. However, professional development programs often look past them when looking for presenters of internal programs.

What's in this for me anyway? or How does this apply to my classroom?

Many scholars explore the extent that programs meet the purpose of effective faculty development. Premises of what effective faculty development should be is generally along the line of what Murray (2001) includes in six categories:

- A climate that fosters and encourages faculty development

- A formalized, structured, and goal-directed development program

- A connection between faculty development and the reward structure

- Faculty ownership

- Colleagues' support for investments in teaching

- The belief that good teaching is valued by administrators.

These key premises would be more complete by adding the context of adult learning to this list.

Brookfield (1994) offered a case study of a presentation to 1000 principals and assistant principals of NYC public schools about staff professional development programs. Within that case study he provided a set of general principles for designing a staff development program:

- Make public the object of the training exercise, the criteria for success, and the needs identified as important

- Involve staff members at all stages of the training process

- Always be flexible and adaptable

- Don't crucify yourself on the cross of perfection

- Ground your exercises in real life issues and concerns

- Be your own methodologist; don't be afraid to use a do-it-yourself approach

He also provided a set of methods for delivery:

- Concentrate on specific skills; don't be theoretical

- The exercises should develop identified skills in real life settings

- The training sessions should be participatory

- The training exercise should allow for frequent, but informative, formative evaluation.

Brookfield's (1994) treatment of staff development includes principles of adult learning without explicitly identifying them as such. Of the bullets in the lists all but one of them, don't crucify yourself on the cross of perfection, parallel adult learning theory.

Lawler and King (2000) say: "the more faculty members can see application to their situations, the more positive their experience with the program will be" (p.94). Supporting this is another premise from the Honolulu Community College (2003) paper stating that adults have a problem-centered orientation to learning.

Table 1 is a chart compiled by Fitzgibbon (2002) of Malcolm Knowles (1970) concepts of pedagogy and andragogy. The category "Orientation to Learning" describes what adults perceive as important in learning; i.e., they are life- task- or problem-centered in their orientation toward learning. Adults will learn something to the extent that they perceive that it will help them deal with problems that they confront in their lives.

Table 1
Andragogical Model vs.
Pedagogical Model of Assumptions

Pedagogical Model	Andragogical Model
The Need to Know	
Learners only need to know that they must learn what the teacher teaches if they want to pass and get promoted; they do not need to know how what they learn will apply to their lives.	Adults need to know why they need to learn something before undertaking to learn it. When adults choose to learn on their own they will expend tremendous energy probing into the benefits of learning it and the consequences of not learning it.
The Learner's Self-Concept	
The teacher's concept of the learner is that of a dependent personality; therefore, the learner's self concept eventually becomes that of a dependent personality.	Adults have a self-concept of being responsible for their own decisions, for their own lives. Therefore, adults have a "psychological need" for self-direction of the learning process.
The Role of Learner's Experience	
The learner's experience is of little worth as a resource for learning; the experience that counts is that of the teacher, the textbook writer, and the audio-visual aids the producer. Therefore, transmittal techniques - lectures, assigned readings,	Adults have both a greater volume and a different quality of experience from youths. Therefore, a wide range of individual differences.

etc., are the backbone of pedagogical methodology.	
Readiness to Learn	
Learners become ready to learn what the teacher tells them they must learn if they want to pass ands get promoted.	Adults become ready to learn those things they need to know and be able to do in order to cope effectively with their real-life situations.
Orientation to Learning	
Learners have a subject-centered orientation to learning; they see learning as acquiring subject-matter content. Therefore, learning experiences are organized according to the logic of the subject-matter content.	Adults are life-centered or task-centered or problem-centered in their orientation toward learning. Adults are motivated to learn something to the extent that they perceive that it will help them perform tasks or deal with problems that they confront in their life situations.
Motivation	
Learners are motivated to learn by external motivators - grades, the teachers' approval or disapproval, parental pressures.	While adults are responsive to some external motivators, the most potent motivators are internal pressures.

Fitzgibbon (2002, p. 35) from Knowles (1990 pp. 55-63)

I can learn this faster on my own. Why can't I just get the materials?

Self-directed learning is a hallmark of the adult learning style. Coupled with the threat possibilities as described earlier, this question jumps to the forefront. The design of faculty development programs and centers is relatively new. The 1970's saw a tremendous growth of these programs (Bakutes, 1998). Alfano (1993) highlights "workshops on instructional skills, advanced teaching and activating learning in the classroom" (p. 71) as primary deliverables.

Faculty development centers often focus on orienting faculty to the institution (Bakutes, 1998). Beyond that she adds that centers help faculty become better teachers rather than focus on discipline-related development. The opportunity for faculty to come together to discuss pedagogy informally in a faculty development center is an asset in itself.

In order to provide these services, centers and programs employ staff and have growing budgets. Murray (1999) challenges colleges to ensure that comprehensive, systemic approaches to faculty development are followed.

In summarizing thoughts from writers in the field, Conti (1983) states "curriculum should be learner centered, that learning episodes should capitalize on the learner's experience, that adults are self-directed, that the learner should participate in needs diagnosis, goals formation, and outcomes evaluation, that adults are problem centered, and that the teacher should serve as a facilitator rather than a repository of facts" (pp. 2-3).

Cross (1981, p. 192) presents the material listed in Table 2 below. The table is based on the work of Penland on why people prefer To learn on their own instead of taking a course.

Table 2
Why people Prefer to learn on their Own

	Catagory	Most Important (percent)
1	Desire to set my own learning pace	46.8
2	Desire to use my own style of learning	37.4
3	I wanted to keep the learning strategy flexible and easy to change	31.0
4	Desire to put my own structure on the learning project	27.8
5	I wanted to learn this right away and couldn't wait until a class might start	36.2
6	I didn't know of any class that taught what I wanted to know	29.8
7	I don't like a formal classroom situation with a teacher	14.0
8	Lack of time to engage in a group learning program	17.9
9	Transportation to a class is to hard or expensive.	5.3
10	I don't have enough money to sign up for a course	5.2

Faculty development programs would likely be more appealing to the faculty by addressing these needs for self-direction. Merriam and Caffarella (1999) describe how self-directed models can be integrated into programs and activities. Three types of models discussed are linear models, interactive models, and instructional models. Reviewing these models will help in including a self-directed mode in faculty development programs and once again cater to the faculty member as an adult learner.

CONCLUSIONS

Lindeman's early seminal work summarized by Knowles, Holton, and Swanson (1998) provides five key assumptions about adult learners

1. Adults are motivated to learn as they experience needs and interests that learning will satisfy

2. Adults' orientation to learning is life-centered

3. Experience is the richest source for adults' learning

4. Adults have a deep need to be self-directing

5. Individual differences among people will increase with age (p. 40)

Brookfield (1994) provides "four characteristics of adult learners—their special orientation to learning, their experiential base, their particular developmental changes and tasks, and their anxiety regarding learning" (p. 30). He later indicated that the concept that adult teaching should be grounded in adult's experiences and that these experiences represent a valuable resource, is generally accepted by adult educators (Brookfield, 1995).

Polson (1993) describes adult learners:

- Occasionally adult students will react emotionally and become defensive when "their truths" are questioned

- Adults have developed some preconceptions

- Programs must ensure a non-threatening learning environment

Faculty could easily replace adult in all of these descriptions. Applying the above principles would provide a response to all of the questions raised in this section.

Overall, what is being discussed here is meeting the needs of faculty learners. As Cross (1981) found "As many as 70 to 80 percent of respondents say that they prefer to learn by some method other than classroom lectures. Nevertheless, lectures usually rank first or second in overall popularity out of the five to ten methods that are generally presented in questionnaires" (p. 208). As acknowledged by many experts in the field, we tend to do things as we learned them or were shown them, rather than following the research evidence of what produces successful learners.

In this paper, a special effort has been made to remind readers that there may be other and better methods to help faculty learn than traditional methods. Applying the principles enumerated in this paper to the design of professional development programs could improve the pedagogy of the delivery and be more likely to attract and retain faculty learners. However, there is no need to change everything in program development and delivery, but rather to adopt adult principles appropriately.

REFERENCES

Alfano, K. (1993). Recent strategies for faculty and staff development. *Community College Review, 21*(1), 68-78.

Bakutes, A. P. (1998).   An examination of faculty development centers. *Contemporary Education, 69*(3), 168-172.

Brawer, F. B. (1990). Faculty development: The literature. *Community College Review, 18*(1), 50-57.

Brookfield, S. D. (1994). *Understanding and facilitating adult learning: A comprehensive analysis of principles and effective practices.* San Francisco: Jossey-Bass.

Brookfield, S. D. (1995). Adult learning an overview. In A. Tuinjman (Ed.), *International Encyclopedia of Education.* Oxford, UK: Pergamon Press. Retrieved October 25, 2003 from http://www.nl.edu/ace/Resources/Documents/ AdultLearning.html.

Conti, G. J. (1983). *Principles of adult learning scale: Follow-up and factor analysis.* Proceedings of the 24th Annual Adult Education Research Conference, Montreal. (Eric Document Reproduction Service No. ED228 424).

Cross, K. P. (1981). *Adults as learners: Increasing participation and facilitating learning.* San Francisco: Jossey-Bass.

Elliot, D. L., Skeff, K. M., & Stratos, G. A. (1999). How do you get to the improvement of teaching? A longitudinal faculty development program for medical educators. *Teaching and Learning in Medicine, 11*(1), 52-57.

Fitzgibbon, S. F. (2002). Assessment of a professional development workshop: Facilitating adult learning. *Dissertations Abstract International, 64*(1) 111A.

Gaff, J. G. (1975). *Toward faculty renewal: Advances in faculty, instructional, and organizational development.* San Francisco: Jossey-Bass, Inc.

Honolulu Community College. (2003). *Principles of adult learning,* Retrieved October 25, 2003, from http://www.hcc.hawaii.edu/intranet/committees/ FacDevCom/guidebk/teachtip/adults-1.htm

Knowles, M. S. (1970). *The modern practice of adult education: Andragogy vs. pedagogy.* New York: Association Press.

Knowles, M. S. (1990). *The adult learner: A neglected species* (4th ed.). Houston: Gulf Publishing.

Knowles, M. S., Holton, E. F., & Swanson, R. A. (1998). *The adult learner: The definitive classic in adult education and human resource development* (5th ed.). Houston: Gulf Publishing.

Lawler, P. A., & King, K. P. (2000). *Planning for effective faculty development: Using adult learning strategies.* Malabar, Florida: Krieger Publishing.

Manzo, K.K. (1996). Faculty development moving in the right direction. *Community College Week, 9*(2), 10-12.

Merriam, S. B., & Caffarella, R. S. (1999). *Learning in adulthood: A comprehensive guide* (2nd ed.). San Francisco: Jossey-Bass.

Millis, B.J. (1994). Faculty development in the 1990s: What it is and why we can't wait. *Journal of Counseling and Development, 72,* 454-464.

Murray, J. P. (1999). Faculty development in a national sample of community colleges. *Community College Review, 27*(3), 47-64.

Murray, J. P. (2001). Faculty development in publicly supported 2-Year colleges. *Community College Journal of Research & Practice, 25*(7), 487-502.

Oromaner, M. (1998). *Faculty and staff development.* ERIC digest (Report No. EDO-JC-98-07). ERIC Clearinghouse for Community Colleges, Los Angeles, CA. (ERIC Document Reproduction Services No. ED 416941).

Polson, C. J. (1993). *Teaching adult students* (Idea Paper No. 29). Manhattan, KS: Center for Faculty Evaluation & Development, Division of Continuing Education, Kansas State University.

FIELD STUDIES WITH STUDENTS

MAKING REAL-WORLD DISCOVERIES

Derek Madden
Modesto College
Diane Grayson
University of South Africa

INTRODUCTION

Promising, as it may appear at first glance, environmental field study can be difficult to teach because of the interdisciplinary breadth and uncertain outcomes that are typical for this approach to learning. Some of the standard curricula used for studying science are inappropriate for environmental field study (Dillon, 2002). What often results when teachers plan environmental education are experiences in which students are not given the opportunity to allow complex issues to be contextualized and discussed (Grace & Ratcliffe, 2002).

Most teachers realize the importance of involving their students in real-world situations, but the instructional experience typically resembles worksheet or walking tour formats. Such activities are driven by packaged curricula that provide teachers ways of measuring learning outcomes on potentially chaotic events such as field studies. Yet, there are missed opportunities for students to make their own discoveries and contribute something that benefits the planet (Hidi,1990; Wellnitz et al., 2002). Real-world experiences in field studies may also foster integrative thinking skills, as students use various learning processes while working towards common goals (Burgess et al., 1999; Orr, 1999).

An authentic field study being explored here involves students' group projects that focus near the base of ecological food chains. This approach contrasts with common practices of nature field study that target large, strange, or interesting animals. These topics of study may initially attract the interests of students; however, the fascination may not translate into high student performance in field study experiences. Lesson plans that focus on plants may allow direct experiences and manipulation of the topic of study, and lead students to perceive numerous connections in nature.

THE STUDY

Student participants were randomly assigned to field study topics and were given introductions on scientific study. Field methods were based on published work, so that students avoided some of the technical problems associated with novel research (Wimmers, 2001).

Following an introduction to basic scientific methods and field study the teaching staff served as participant observers that rotated their position on the field study groups (Aubusson, 2002). Students worked cooperatively in groups as they applied the inquiry method to investigate a specific problem and gather data. Student groups worked in a double blind situation, with each group studying at a different tier of the food chain in relation to the shared research topic. Field projects were available to participants without any screening for race, creed, and religion, through a post-secondary, educational organization called The School for Field Studies. The field study site was situated on the Pacific coast of Costa Rica. The study was conducted at Playa Ostional during the peak turtle nesting period, and involved 41 first and second year college students working in the field for three months.

The students' group investigation reports were measured through performance-based assessment to determine the achievement level (Bentley et al., 2000). This involved stages of holistic scoring of student group reports that fit within research guidelines originally established by the research staff (Table 1). These guidelines for scoring the group papers were presented to the students before the group projects commenced.

Table 1
Guidelines for Student Field Research Papers

Category	Description
Multidisciplinary	Human social, political, or cultural conditions are addressed as a consideration of the study.
Application	The paper concludes with sound recommendations for how the results may be used to benefit the organism being studied, the environment, human conditions, or the planet
Need for study	Through literature review and referral to the results, the paper makes a convincing argument that this study is important
Quality	The scientific method is employed in a manner that reduces the potential for bias and errors that influence the results.

Environmental field projects involving student groups were planned 16 months prior to the actual fieldwork. In a feasibility study, the proposed research site was examined in regards to logistics, safety and its potential interest to visitors (Deng, et al., 2002). The research question was matched with the study site to examine the potential for impact on, or improvement of the environment (Gibbs, 1998; Van der Dium & Caalders, 2002). The student groups worked in a two-independent-groups design, under similar conditions in the field (Table 2). Student teams each had equal access to necessary equipment, literature and logistic support (McGuigan 1997).

Table 2
Stepping-Stones in Generating the Field Projects

Step	Description
1. Topic.	Teaching staff consults experts for research topics with potential for completion. Literature gathered for each research topic provides information, methods, and links to the proposed project.
2. Site consideration.	Location of the study conforms to safety requirements established by the educational institutions. Experts that have worked at the site are consulted prior to approval of the study site.

| 3. Field research. | Methods are proposed that involve few hazardous materials. Field equipment must be durable and not require extensive training prior to use. Participants are randomly assigned to a research topic. Each group of participants works in the field as a team under the guidance of a research staff or intern researcher. |
| 4. Project report | Participants work from shared data that their group acquired through field study. Although data is shared, each member of the group produces their own written research report that contains an introduction, methods, results and discussion. |

At the conclusion of their research projects, participants orchestrated their knowledge and followed the four guidelines to produce a report about their field discoveries. Student group papers were presented in a mini-symposium and the papers were scored as if they were being submitted for publication (Table 3). Standards for the student group paper acceptance were at an appropriate level for an introductory college course in biology. Field staff scored each group paper based on the four guidelines. These scorers were not aware of the independent variable (base of food chain) being examined in this study.

Table 3
Student Project Assessment Tools

Assessment tool	Personnel	Scoring & Analysis
Internal juried review of student projects	Research staff and interns help guide student projects. First and second year college students fulfill 3 units of biology by taking the field study course.	I. Holistic scoring of student papers: 3. Accepted as is 2. Accepted with major revision required 1. Rejected II. Statistical T-test: $t = \dfrac{x - u}{s / \sqrt{n}}$

FINDINGS

After three months of field studies with students from various colleges in the US and Costa Rica, several significant differences were observed between the control student groups and those studying at the base of food chains. The greatest differences were revealed for groups in the area of application and establishing a need for the study (Table 4).

Students studying at the base of food chains were able to gather enough data in their field study to run statistical tests and produce charts. These students were observed to manipulate their study topics, taking samples back to the research station for further studying. Through amassing substantial data, students studying at the base of food chains were able to establish the impact of vegetation on sea turtle nesting. Turtles that came ashore successfully nested in beach sand in 92% of the attempts (excluding what are known as false nesting crawls). Successful nesting in sand that was vegetated by Abronia spp. and other stolon-producing plants reduced sea turtle nesting success to 34%.

Table 4
Results for Student Field Research Papers (n = 41) at Ostional, Costa Rica

Category	Major trends	Scoring statistics
Multidisciplinary	Both student groups made progress towards understanding human connections with the sea turtles.	Control = 2.43 ± 1.7 Food chain base = 2.70 ± 2.0 Not significant (NS)
Application	Students studying at the base of food chains acquired a substantial amount of data that allowed them to make recommendations on how their results may be used to improve the sea turtles' situation as an endangered species.	Control = 1.20 ± 1.3 Food chain base = 2.45 ± 2.0 P < .01
Need for study	Both sets of papers had good introductions, based largely on readings and lectures. Students studying at the base of food chains were able to use their ample data to make convincing arguments establishing a need for the field study.	Control = 1.54 ± 1.0 Food chain base = 2.4 ± 0.9 P < .05
Quality	No significant difference was revealed in the scoring or observed trends in the quality of either control or food chain based student papers	Control = 2.15 ± 1.4 Food chain base = 2.3 ± 1.7 NS

Students that directly studied the sea turtles and the animals that interacted with the reptiles, experienced long periods in which data acquisition was difficult. Turtle nesting occurred mostly at night, and even then there were many nights when no turtles were observed to nest at all. This left students searching for other animals to study, which tended to lead students to make assumptions based on very little objective data. Students studying the turtles found it most productive to observe the activity of known predators of sea turtles, which prey upon turtle hatchlings. Data from this approach were meager, and the group research papers reflected this weakness in the results and discussion sections.

CONCLUSIONS AND RECOMMENDATIONS

The way in which field studies are conducted with students has powerful implications. In this study, students studying the base of natural food chains performed well in all areas of the course objectives. This success was not experienced to the same extent in the control group, which focused their energies on studying sea turtles.

Part of the discrepancy between the experimental and control groups may lie in the importance of being able to study a topic that is readily available for examination and manipulation. The base of the food chain group kept themselves busy studying how plants might relate to the nesting success of sea turtles. Their activities included extensive walking, digging, and measuring. Data acquired were like a paycheck that could be applied to something else, in this case it was graphs that supported their paper.

The groups that studied turtles often came away from several hours of research with no substantial data, which resulted in dismal results sections in their papers. The working assumption, based on the work of others, is that students prefer to be involved in learning situations where they are contributing something meaningful (Wellnitz et al., 2002).

Field explorations can result in scientific discoveries that address environmental problems, and sometimes novice researchers help these discoveries to happen (Greengrove & Secord, 2003). However, studying animals directly may be best left to scientists with the fortitude and funding to expend large amounts of unproductive time on animal field studies. Teachers typically require fast and organized ways for field studies to proceed, so that students are kept on task and the outcomes can be objectively scored.

Field explorations may have the potential for success when bases of food chains are examined as they relate to animals. Plants, algae and other such organisms are typically abundant and, when the project is planned appropriately, can be linked to a more "exciting" organism such as a sea turtle.

The results from this paper may cause some teachers to rethink their field trip lesson plans. Rather than directing field studies on conspicuous animals, teachers may involve students in studying the base of food chains. Instead of a standard field trip involving worksheets or tours, teachers may look for ways for students to investigate real problems. The potential is there for students to make discoveries, to contribute and to be objectively measured for grading purposes when involved in field explorations.

REFERENCES

Aubusson, P. (2002). Ecology of science education. *International Journal of Science Education, 24*, 27-46.

Bentley, M., Ebert, C., & Ebert, E. (2000). *The natural investigator*. Belmont, CA: Wadsworth.

Burgess, A., Caslavka, C., & Howell, E. (1999). Connecting student learning with real problems: The biocore prairie project. *Bioscene: Journal of College Biology Teaching, 25*, 3-6.

Deng, J., King, B., & Bauer, T. (2002). Evaluation natural attractions for tourism. *Annals of Tourism, 29*, 422-438.

Dillon, J. (2002). Editorial-perspectives on environmental education-related research in science education. *International Journal of Science Education, 24*,1111-1117.

Gibbs, J. P. (1998). *Problem solving in conservational biology and wildlife management.* New York: Blackwell Science.

Grace, M. M., & Ratcliffe, M. (2002). The science and values that young people draw upon to make decisions about biological conservation issues. *International Journal of Science Education, 11*, 1157-1169.

Greengrove, C., & Secord, D. (2003). Undergraduate marine research. *Journal of College Science Teaching, 32*,316-321.

Hidi, S. (1990). Interest and its contribution as a mental resource for learning. *Review of Educational Research, 60*, 549-572.

McGuigan, F. J. (1997). *Experimental psychology: Methods of research.* Englewood Cliffs, NJ: Prentice Hall.

Orr, D.W. (1999). Education, careers, and callings: The practice of conservation biology. *Conservation Biology, 13*,1242-1245.

Van der Duim, R., & Caalders, J (2002). Biodiversity and tourism impact and interventions. *Annals of Tourism, 29,* 743-761.

Wellnitz, T., MacRury, N., Child, A., & Bensons, D. (2002). Spreading the wealth: Graduate students and educational outreach. *Conservation Biology, 16,* 560-563.

Wimmers, L. (2001). Practicing real science in the laboratory: A project-based approach to teaching microbiology. *Journal of College Science Teaching, 31,* 167-171.

NEW QUALITY BENCHMARKS

FOR ONLINE COURSES:

MESHING TECHNOLOGY

AND CONCEPTUAL UNDERPINNING

Susan S. Nash
University of Oklahoma

INTRODUCTION

Quality benchmarks have been established for Internet-based programs in higher education. In addition there have been numerous articles and publications that deal with what are considered to be the essential elements in a high-quality online course. However, ideas are constantly evolving in response to changing technology, learner needs, and institutional goals.

A review of current practice, combined with a literature review reveals a number of commonly-held beliefs and protocols. However, what is *not* clear is to what degree the recommendations are being implemented in actual practice. Further, it is far from self-evident how attitudes may be shifting and new trends emerging. Because of the ever-expanding base of individuals and groups who need to have the best possible understanding of what factors to take into consideration when developing an online course or e-learning experience, a new survey instrument and results that it yields could be very useful.

This paper reports on the development of such a survey instrument. While other instruments, such as the one published by the Institute for Higher Education Policy

(2000) seek to look at the entire program and include such broad categories as institutional context, student support, faculty training and support, infrastructure, curriculum and instruction, this instrument looks primarily at curriculum and instruction

The goal of the instrument is two-fold—to provide a checklist of current standards and to gauge shifts in attitudes and ideas about the importance of items. In doing so, emerging trends and practices will reveal themselves as perceived by the various decision-makers and stake-holders in the online course development, implementation, and administration process.

The new instrument, "Online Course Quality Benchmarks" (Nash, 2003) has been designed to be responded to by individuals involved in online education, training, and lifelong learning. Although they work with learner groups possessing unique characteristics, the target group for the survey includes individuals involved in online courses in the following groups: higher education (community colleges, four-year institutions, graduate programs); K-12 academic content providers (home-school and traditional); professional development, training (including military); and lifelong learning.

BACKGROUND

Instruction using the Web as a vehicle for content dissemination and instructor-student interaction has come to dominate distance learning. Beyond the obvious utility in situations where learners are separated from the instructor, the Web is now increasingly utilized for instruction in settings that combine face-to-face instruction with Web-based learning activities done outside the classroom ("blended" or "hybrid" courses). To describe what occurs in the distance component, authors and researchers use the two terms "distance education" and "distance learning" interchangeably (Duvall & Schwartz, 2000; Wolfe, 1996). Within distance learning, a course that is taught almost exclusively via the Web is referred to in a number of ways, but generally as an online course (Montilva, et al., 2002).

The online program is the overall structure within which an online course is incorporated. In the Institute for Higher Education's Policy (2000) on benchmarks for success in online learning, the following categories were used for review:

- Institutional Support

- Course Development

- Teaching/Learning Process

- Course Structure

- Student Support

- Faculty Support

- Evaluation and Assessment

Institutions involved included Brevard Community College, Regents College, University of Illinois at Urbana-Champaign, University of Maryland University College, Utah State University, and Weber State University.

There are numerous approaches to organizing information and tools used in online courses within an online program. Many institutions use commercially-available online course management software such as Blackboard, WebCT, Desire2Learn. Other have adopted open-source software, while others such as MIT have developed their own proprietary course management software.

While it may be tempting to shift the responsibility of course quality to the course management software, the fact remains that the management system is simply a platform and/or an interface. It does not include content, nor do most software providers cue course developers or instructors as to the most effective online learning strategies.

The rapid evolution of course management software, combined with rapid shifts in technology, access, and needs led writers to focus on specific applications rather than the course as a whole. For example, Boling and Frick (1997) look at integration of databases, while Palloff and Pratt (1999) focus on the role of chat, discussion boards, and messaging systems. Others list the elements with which to populate one's online course (using course management software), without much consideration to the course developer's decision-making process (Khan, 1997; O'Sullivan, 1999; Schweizer, 1999).

Most of the literature tends to be limited because it is prescriptive in nature without dealing with the underlying psychological or epistemological issues that make distance learning different than face-to-face. It is because of a perceived need to expand the understanding of how and why decisions are made to include certain elements in a "high-quality" online course that the "Online Course Quality Benchmarks" survey was developed.

Developing a course is more than simply uploading a syllabus, lectures, and taping a few illustrative lectures. Authors such as Hall (1999) and Moore (1997) look at traditional elements, such as the syllabus or the study guide, as a foundation, but their work is limited by being rather dated, and because it was unlikely that many of their suggestions were based on the ideas or responses of individuals with more than just a few years of actual practical experience. In 2003, a full four or five years later, the situation is different, and it is easier to locate online course practitioners with at least three to five years of practical experience.

CURRENT PRACTICE
IN COURSE DEVELOPMENT:
FACULTY-LED VS. INSTITUTION-LED
APPROACHES

Over the last few years, two different approaches to course development and management have emerged: faculty-led course development, vs. department-led course development.

Faculty-led Online Course Development

In this model, the faculty member is responsible for developing the content for the course, as well as the components that are loaded into course management software. The faculty member begins by developing his or her own course, often adapted from one taught on-site in a traditional classroom. The instructor develops instructional materials: typically a syllabus, lecture notes, required work and samples of successful student papers. Discussion boards, announcements, automated assessments (quizzes, etc.), collaborative activities, grade books, and class resources are then configured within the course management software platform, usually WebCT, Blackboard, Prometheus, Desire2Learn, open-source, or proprietary platforms.

Pros. The faculty member can control the content and constantly update, upgrade, and adjust the course and course content. Because control is kept at faculty-level, the documents are likely to be updated more often, and there would be less chance of critical errors.

Cons. Faculty-led course content development is enormously time-consuming and requires the individual to keep up-to-date with software programs and interfaces. It is difficult for a faculty member to build and maintain content for more than one or two courses. Even with substantial technical and instructional design support, the task can be overwhelming.

Department- or Institution-led
Online Course Development

This approach is used by the University of Phoenix, as well as other large distance universities having multiple sections of a single course. Such institutions may also employ a large number of adjuncts or short-term contract instructors. Basically, the department assembles a course development team which may consist of subject matter experts, instructional designers, editors, programmers, graphics specialists, instructional technologists, and team leaders. The team develops a course which includes all the facilitated e-learning elements in the faculty-led course design, but in addition, may incorporate streaming media clips, audio, additional articles, graphics, which can be purchased or licensed for use by the institution.

Once developed, the course is updated on a regular basis. It can take the form of a course content Website, or be saved as a Blackboard (or WebCT) cartridge to be accessed by all the instructors of each section of the course. It can be used for several years, and for hundreds of sections per semester.

Pros. Although the development costs may be high, the long-run cost-effectiveness of this model is impressive, particularly if there are multiple sections and it can be offered for two or three years. The course content is consistent, and the department can be assured that all the students taking the course are receiving the same content, and the same mode of delivery.

Cons. Because the instructors of the course did not develop the course, it is very important to require the faculty to attend training and to understand precisely how they are expected to interact and guide students. The initial development costs can be high, and it is necessary to develop a standard procedure for course development, as well as standard course templates for uniform structure. Because of the standardization, there is a very real danger of approaching a "course in a box" trap, and not offer enough meaningful collaborative activities for the truly individualized instruction to take place. This is particularly the case if the video and course content are "on-demand" there is very little discussion board activity, and it is not possible to e-mail the instructor.

DEVELOPMENT OF THE SURVEY INSTRUMENT

Methodology

Based on a review of literature dealing with e-learning, online course development, and best practices for online programs, the following propositions were proposed for study and form the foundation of the questions and approach used in developing the survey instrument.

Proposition One. In order to assure that there is uniformity in content and quality between courses, it is necessary to provide a consistent guide or checklist of learner items which includes such activities as reading a syllabus, reading text, and engaging in learner activities.

Proposition Two. In order to assure that learning goals are being met, it is necessary to have a recommended procedure or protocol that requires the developer to look at the content being presented and the outcomes desired from the point of view of meaning, knowledge acquisition, and epistemology.

Proposition Three. For an effective course, the developer must bring together learner items with epistemological protocols in ways that systematize knowledge acquisition and synthesis. This can be as simple as a list of questions and approaches to the course design, development and implementation.

Overview of the Survey Instrument

After a literature review, an analysis of the results of smaller surveys, and two online program best-practices reviews, the author developed a survey instrument that incorporated elements of widely-accepted benchmarks (Institute for Higher Education Policy, 2000) and learner-centered technology (Duvall & Schwartz, 2000). Many universities' best practices for authorship and design were examined, including those of the University of Central Florida (1999), University of Tasmania (2002), and Fort Hays State University (2003). It must be noted that most universities' "best practices" consist of lists of activities and items to include. There is little or no discussion of underlying pedagogical, epistemological, or even ideological factors.

An exception can be found in essays on feminist and post-modernist responses to the Internet. Far from the identity reconstruction arena it promised to be in the early days, writers such as Susanna Paasonen (2002) suggest that the Internet does not create a gender-neutral experience. Instead, "gender ceases to be a problem only if women 'act more like men'" (p. 94). Women come to be identified based on their "needs," which tend to be defined by the products they consume. How such patterns impact online courses or education is yet to be seen.

The survey instrument is designed to be taken by individuals who have created or been involved in the online course development process for at least one course. The categories of questions, broken down into sections, are designed to help individuals express the level of importance they ascribe to certain elements or processes. In doing so, they not only delineate their current practice, they also indicate preferences and relative importance. If the survey instrument is administered to the same group at different points of time, the results can be used to track emerging trends and shifts in attitudes in the course development process.

The survey instrument contains sections that correspond to aspects or elements of online course design, development, and administration. A uni-dimensional Likert scale is used for greater precision.

Survey, Section 1: Learning Goals

Because the mediation that occurs in face-to-face environments is not as easily effected in an online course, it is very important to identify and describe the desired learning outcomes. If that does not happen, it is possible that students will become enmeshed in peripheral items. Consistency of outcome, and an ability to classify and remember specific fact-based knowledge will be a primary goal. Another is the goal of assuring that deeper learning is taking place, which would be evidenced in tasks requiring synthesis, creative problem-solving, and conceptual analysis.

In face-to-face instruction, learning goals are often developed and expressed via the Socratic method; that is, through question and answer. This may happen in online courses, via e-mail and threaded discussion boards. However, such evolutionary approaches are often ineffective in an online environment. It has been suggested that expressing the learning objectives at the beginning of the course and at each unit can help students focus (Knox 2002). Others (Henke, 2001) feel that such an approach limits the learners and keeps them from being able to explore the breadth and depth of the content, or to have freedom to apply the concepts to one's own life.

Ragan (1999) stresses that good instruction transcends delivery method, but that in an online environment, practice should follow principles, because opportunities for clarification are limited. "Learning goals should be defined as part of the instructional design plan. Once defined, they should be publicly available and communicated clearly and explicitly to the student in whatever manner suits the design model—in print, face to face, or via a web site" (p. 3).

The questions in this section have been designed to address how learning goals are structured, and how they refer to the kinds of knowledge and learning outcomes that are encompassed in the course.

Survey Questions on Learning Goals. The following are included in the instrument:

1---Does the course include a list of overall learning objectives?
2---Does the course syllabus or Website describe how the learner will achieve the objectives?
3---Are the learning objectives clear?
4---Do the learning goals include synthesis of course-spanning material?
5---Do the learning goals include mastery of declarative knowledge involving specific content?
6---Are there learning goals for each unit?

Survey, Section 2: Content

The instructor or course facilitator in an online course must plan the delivery of content in an online course. In a face-to-face environment, content can be modified, challenged, and spontaneously delivered in response to questions. In an online environment, planning content is important in order make certain that the depth, breadth, and level match the needs and abilities of the learners, in addition to making certain they have access to information and activities needed to achieve learning goals.

Questions regarding content and whether or not it is appropriate for Web-based delivery are considered to be the first step in the development of an online course by many writers (Chow & Shutters, 2002; McAlister, Rivera, & Hallam, 2001). These questions are usually initially addressed by faculty, although decisions are often made at the department or college level (Roberson & Klotz, 2002).

Content questions in the survey instrument are closely linked to an awareness of structured learning goals and instructional design. However, the focus expands to include the collaborative nature of some online course development procedures. The instrument should reveal attitudes and current practice with respect to a course content review process.

Survey Questions on Content. The following are included in the instrument:

7---Does the online course include the right amount of content to be able to achieve all the learning objectives?
8---Does a person other than the instructor review course materials to be assured of the quality of course materials?
9---Is the content of the course easily covered in the time frame required by the course?
10---Is the course content at the right educational level for the learner?

11---Is the course content variable so that students wishing enrichment or additional reading can easily find it, either in the online course itself, or in easily accessible libraries or resource centers?

Survey, Section 3: Instructional Design

While informal instructional design has always played a part in face-to-face learning, in previous delivery-modes there has been a reliance on an apprenticeship model in which master teachers share their pedagogy and approaches. Although shadowing and mentoring are important, the online environment requires the construction of a learning space far in anticipation of the actual activity. In order to be effective, instructional design tasks have to be formalized and there should be an ongoing awareness of how and why decisions are made. Best practices will evolve over time in response to learner needs.

Henke (2001) writes extensively on the elements of instructional design that should be taken into consideration in an online course, and that "the critical factor to the success of web based instruction is the incorporation of usability design into the development process" (p. 6). In the University of Central Florida's (1999) "Best Practices for Authorship, Design and Website Management," a prescriptive approach is taken with suggestions segmented into considerations—browser, reader/printing, navigation, and others. Although this is convenient, such an approach is likely to be ephemeral due to the quickly evolving nature of technology and instructional practice.

The questions in this survey instrument try to assess whether or not there is a deeper understanding of the underlying principles. Procedures are good, but if designers and course developers do not grasp the more universal concepts, there is likely to be a problem.

The questions in the survey instrument also rephrase items in the section on learning goals in order to see if there are inconsistencies in responses, and to reveal when goals are understood in different ways, depending upon the context.

Survey Questions on Instructional Design. The following are included in the instrument:

12---Is the course designed in such a way that the learning goals are made clear?

13---Are specific activities developed that center on each learning goal?

14---Are learners presented with more than one way (or activity) to achieve a learning goal in order to accommodate multiple learning styles?

15---Are activities designed in a way to require faculty to respond with guidance and coaching?

16---Do instructors have a chance to modify the course content or activities?

17---Do graphics reinforce course content and help students make connections and/or illustrate learning goals?

18---Does the course management software have an integrated function that allows students to do more than one thing while logged into a single site, such as engage in a discussion board or online chat, send e-mail, submit work, access course documents, participate in group projects, and/or contact the professor?

19---Does the course management software work well over a modem connection?

20---Can a student log into the course management software from an Internet café, military computer lab, or office where there are strict firewalls?

Survey, Section 4: Interactivity

Many studies have demonstrated that student success in an online course depends on the level and quality of interaction. Interactivity in an online course can take many forms, ranging from automatic responses generated by applets, to human interaction in discussion areas or via e-mail. The guidance provided by interactivity not only keeps a learner focused on overall objectives, it also is a factor in motivation.

For some course developers and theorists such as Edelstein and Edwards (2002), interactivity in the form of threaded discussion boards is the key to successful learning. They pay special attention to the way in which questions are structured and responses are guided and indicate that this form of interaction is crucial to the development of learning communities.

Others, such as the Sloan Consortium (Sloan-C, 2002), tend to look at the threaded discussion as a part of an overall matrix of course and online instruction elements. These key practice areas include assessment, course design, interaction, learning outcomes, learning resources, and pedagogy. An effective online course does incorporate interaction. The interaction can be between and among students and between students and instructor, as well as student interaction with course content.

Hricko (2002) writes that "students' frustrations with web-based courses originated from minimal and not timely feedback and from ambiguous instructions on the website as well as through e-mail" (p. 7). This observation is underscored by numerous studies and from the author's personal experience. Because of potential ambiguity, the survey instrument questions focus on procedure rather than perceptions of community.

Survey Questions on Interactivity. The following are included in the instrument:

21---Is the learner engaged through the opportunity for input to automated programs?
22---Is the learner engaged through interaction with other students in a virtual classroom or learning community?
23---Is the learner engaged in one-on-one communication or interaction with the instructor?
24---Does the instructor have an opportunity to modify or customize interactive tasks, such as discussion board topics?

Survey, Section 5: Navigation

Learners are frustrated when they find themselves lost in the course and cannot find help to make their way in an ordered, understandable manner. Navigation is not simply a matter of providing links. It also involves efficiencies and ease of access. In a course requiring more than three links where students are accessing via modems on phone connections, their connection time is likely to be slow. Course management software that requires frequent logins and multiple screens to access a single point is one such problem. This introduces another level of frustration. Navigation is a key component, but often overlooked in course management and design.

Lazonder (2003) has found that novice and experienced Web users have different approaches toward searching for information. Experienced users are likely to have more patience in their searches, and will persist with more attempts. Yet, they are also less likely to follow specific instructions or online tutorials. These are important when developing "intuitive" navigation guides.

Survey Questions on Navigation. The following are included in the instrument:

25---Can users easily determine how to find the syllabus, required work, e-mail, discussion board, content and course activities in the course?
26---Are there navigation buttons to library or other online resources?
27---Is there a navigation button for help with the course management system?
28---Is the course designed so that the pages load rapidly after the navigation buttons are clicked?
29---Is there a navigation button that shows learners how to submit their work?
30---Can access to key information or activities be accomplished in three clicks (screens) or less?
31---Is there a course map?
32---Are the icons and/or clear labels intuitive enough that a learner can learn by doing, rather than having to read user manuals or excessive documentation?

Survey, Section 6: Motivational Components

Without taking motivation into consideration, online courses are likely to fail. Motivation does not simply involve the learner. It also involves the instructor, who, if not properly motivated, will not follow through in tasks required for student success. What motivates some learners will de-motivate others. For that reason, it is important to understand learners' needs and backgrounds and develop motivational components with those elements in mind.

Ehrmann (1995) writes that "the medium is not the message. Communications media and other technologies are so flexible that they do not dictate methods of teaching and learning" (p. 6). He emphasizes trying to identify which teaching strategies are best and matching them with the technologies best for supporting those strategies.

Teaching strategies should include a needs assessment as well as an analysis of the target audience to make sure that the motivational strategies are appropriate and likely to be effective. Continuing to emphasize the importance of foregrounding the educational experience rather than relying on the technology for intrinsic motivation, Ehrmann (1995) continues: "What matters most are educational strategies for using technology, strategies that can influence the student's total course of study" (p. 9).

Motivation connects directly to utility. For example, the Navy's e-learning program helped prepare reservists for deployment. "Naval reservists, like their active duty counterparts, are able to logon to the Navy e-learning site and complete courses to enrich both their military training as well as their civilian careers" (Maskell, 2003, p. 4).

Questions in the survey instrument overlap and connect with other sections, including learning goals, instructional design, interactivity, and use of media. The rationale for the cross-over is the notion that certain elements impact motivation—community building, responsiveness, game/entertainment, intrinsic motivators, connections to career or real-life applications.

Survey Questions on Motivation. The following are included in the instrument:

33---Does the course engage the user through novelty, humor, game elements, testing, adventure, unique content, surprise elements, etc.?
34---Has a learner needs assessment been conducted to assure that course activities give the learner an opportunity to make connections to his or her own interests or goals?
35---Do course activities clearly seem relevant to achieving learning objectives?

36---Do course activities help prepare learners to better deal with situations they will encounter in the real world?

37---Is the instructor charged with providing timely feedback?

38---Is the instructor required to provide substantive feedback, such as guidance, suggestions, revision requirements, corrections of fact, encouragements to look at more than one side of an issue?

39---Are students guided and encouraged to directly respond to other learners in threaded discussion boards?

40---Has information been gathered about the learners to assure that the motivational components are effective, culturally appropriate, and not offensive?

41---Are required texts and course materials of high quality? Are they up to date?

42---Is the instructor required to participate in training that includes how to provide positive motivation to learners?

43---Are incentives or rewards provided for excellence in online instruction?

Survey, Section 7: Use of Media

The use of streaming media in online learning can be invaluable, particularly in subject matter areas that have a performance aspect. These include languages, film studies, medicine, engineering, sports, etc. It can also be a good source of illustrative content. However, if badly implemented and designed, media can be distracting and so cumbersome that access is not realistically possible. The use of media—from both instructional design and technology points of view—must be carefully designed and implemented.

Chisholm (2003) emphasizes the role of media in simulation and skill acquisition, as well as higher-order synthesis and decision-making tasks:

In the command-and-control vehicle, a soldier will have to understand and act on diverse pieces of information provided by unmanned aerial vehicles, scout vehicle/sensor video, satellites, human assets and other information-gathering mechanisms. The job will be so cognitively challenging that the premium on training and skill level will be greater than ever. More extensive tactical decision-making instruction and practice will be required in order to make Future Combat System (FCS) feasible (p. 1).

Although Chisholm is writing about military applications, he mentions that such approaches are also used in universities and in professional training. The survey instrument questions ask the respondent to identify how and where the media is used and to reveal if conscious decisions are made to avoid gratuitous or distracting media applications. Online course developers can become so engrossed in mastering the software that they forget the overall learning goals and objectives. The survey instrument questions address that concern as well.

Survey Questions on Use of Media. The following are included in the instrument:

44---Does the course appropriately and effectively employ graphics, animation, music, sound, video, etc.?
45---Is the gratuitous use of these media avoided?
46---Does the software used for streaming media accommodate different connection speeds, including modems?
47---Does the media encourage interactive learning?
48---Does the media feature a "talking head" or a tape of a professor delivering a lecture in a typical traditional classroom?
49---Is the music or soundtrack annoying?

Survey, Section 8: Evaluation

In order to determine whether or not learners are achieving goals and objectives, it is necessary to develop methods of assessing and evaluating their progress. Many writers (Chickering & Reisser, 1993; Reeves, 2002; Rosenberg, 2001) approach online evaluation in the same way they would in a traditional face-to-face learning environment. However, Angelo and Cross (1993) describe how overuse of evaluation can be de-motivating. Obviously, finding the right balance is very important.

Many writers (Huba and Freed, 1999) encourage thinking of e-learning as outcomes. Reeves (2002) states:

> Mental models are important cognitive structures that influence how we react to change and solve problems...Rather than as technologies, activities, or content collections, a mental model of e-learning can be based upon the concept of 'outcomes.' Outcomes are achieved objectives; they are the evidence that learning has occurred, performance has changed, and the results have been attained (p. 7).

Evaluation in this survey instrument deals with e-learner performance evaluation and assessment. The questions ask the respondent to think about the way a student is evaluated as well as the intellectual content.

Survey Questions on Evaluation. The following are included in the instrument:

51---Are learners evaluated following the completion of a simulation?
52---Are learners evaluated or assessed after the completion of writing activities?

53---Do learners receive grades or assessments after completing a research activity?
54---Must learners demonstrate mastery of each section's content before proceeding to later sections?
55---Do learners have section quizzes?
56---Is there a final exam?

Survey, Section 9: Aesthetics

Aesthetics have to do with the overall look and feel of the online course. Although aesthetics may play a role in traditional face-to-face learning, usually the appearance of a presentation, or the aesthetics of the overall learning experience are not as important as in the online environment, where distracting designs and colors can have a negative impact on the student. Aesthetics include issues of semiotics, signs, symbols, and arrangement—all the non-textual elements that generate meaning and interpretive possibilities.
Survey Questions on Aesthetics. The following are included in the instrument

57---Is the interface design attractive and appealing to the eye and ear?
58---Are the graphics stimulating?
59---Is the course evaluated by more than one person in order to determine whether or not graphics or design could be offensive or culturally inappropriate?
60---Is the course navigation element designed so that it does not create a distraction?

Survey, Section 10: Record Keeping

Without clear and consistent record-keeping, students and instructors quickly become frustrated and errors are made. Privacy laws must be respected, and security is a must. The online environment requires administrators and designers to re-think record keeping. Students like to know where they stand and to start from where they left off.

Survey Questions on Record Keeping. The following are included in the instrument:

61---Are student performance data recorded, such as time to complete, grades on activities, question analyses, and final scores?
62---Are scores or grades communicated directly to the student?
63---Are grades posted in an online gradebook?
64---Is the site secure?

Survey, Section 11: Tone or Ethos

The tone of a site relates a great deal to the tone of a written document or a media presentation. It encompasses the "voice" that comes through in the situation. Generally stated, "ethos" has to do with credibility, and is closely related to ethics, character, and believability. Both are vitally important in the online environment. If tone and ethos are problematic, the validity of the information, the approach, and the instructor can be seriously compromised.

The course developer must understand the needs of the learners, as well as their dominant characteristics in order to construct an e-learning environment that possesses the right tone or ethos. Otherwise there may be significant variations of usability.

Henke (2001) and Nielsen (1996) suggest that technical issues are only one part of design flaws. They suggest in their "Top Ten Web Design Mistakes" that lack of navigation support, long scrolling pages and outdated information are the result of not understanding how the users are likely to approach the Web course. Further problems occur when there is a lack of understanding of one's audience (language, cultural issues, semiotics, tone).

Tone and ethos-tuning are complicated by the changing dynamics of online learning. Organizational structures are characterized by partnerships and collaborations between traditional universities, businesses, corporate and for-profit training centers, and technology partners (O'Donoghue et al., 2001). Survey instrument questions probe the respondent's awareness of the importance of gathering information about one's potential learners.

Survey Questions on Tone or Ethos. The following are included in the instrument:

65---Is the tone of the writing in the online course appropriate for the audience?
66---Does the tone avoid being condescending, trite, pedantic, etc.?
67---Is the tone consistently positive and encouraging?
68---Does the tone promote a sense of fairness?
69---Is the tone (or "ethos") of the course a consistent one that encourages intellectual risk-taking and intellectual investigation?
70---Does the tone or "ethos" create a supportive environment for making connections between real-world situations and the course content?
71---Does the tone encourage the learner to become emotionally invested in a positive attitude about online learning?

Access To The Survey Instrument

"Online Course Quality Benchmarks" is available online; you're invited to respond to it. Taking the survey requires about 15 minutes. See http://intercom.virginia.edu/ SurveySuite/Surveys/Course_Benchmarks.

REFERENCES

Angelo, T. A., & Cross, P. K. (1993). *Classroom assessment and technologies* (2nd ed.). San Francisco: Jossey-Bass.

Boling, E., & Frick, T. W. (1997). Holistic rapid prototyping for Web design: Early usability testing is essential. In B. H. Khan (Ed.), *Web-based instruction* (pp. 319-328). Englewood Cliffs, NJ: Educational Technology Publications.

Chickering, A., & Reisser, L. (1993). *Education and identity.* San Francisco: Jossey-Bass.

Chisholm, P. (2003). *Tutoring for future combat. Military training technology: Online edition.* Retrieved November 1, 2003, from http://www.mt2-kmi.com/pring_article. cfm?DocID=219.

Chow, O., & Shutters, J. (2002). *Do's and don'ts in offering online developmental math courses.* Harrisburg, PA: Harrisburg Area Community College.

Duvall, C. K., & Schwartz, R. G. (2000). Distance education: Relationship between academic performance and technology-adept adult students. *Education and Information Technologies, 5*(3), 177-187.

Edelstein, S., & Edwards, J. (2002). If you build it, they will come: Building learning communities through threaded discussions. *Online Journal of Distance Learning Administration, 5*(1), 1-9. Retrieved November 11, 2003, from http://www.westga.edu/~distance/ojdla/spring51/ edelstein51.htm.

Ehrmann, S. C. (1995). Asking the right question: What does research tell us about technology and higher learning? *Change*, (27)2, 20-27.

Fort Hays State University. (2003). *AQIP Quality Criteria*. Retrieved December 22, 2003 from http://www. fhsu. edu/aquip/quality_crit.shtml.

Hall, R. H. (1999). Instructional web site design principles: A literature review and synthesis. *The Virtual University Journal. 2*, 1-12.

Henke, H. (2001). *Evaluating web-based instruction design*. Retrieved December 22, 2003, from http://scis.nova.edu/ ~henkeh/ story1.htm.

Hricko, M. (2002). Developing an interactive web-based classroom. *Journal of the Distance Learning Association*. Retrieved December 22, 2003, from http://www.usdla. org/html/ journal/NOV02_Issue/article05.html.

Huba, M. E., & Freed, J. (1999). *Learner-centered assessment on college campuses: Shifting the focus from teaching to learning*. Needham Heights, MA: Allyn & Bacon.

Institute for Higher Education Policy. (2000). *Quality on the line: Benchmarks for success in Internet-based distance education*. Washington, D. C.: Author.

Khan, B. H. (1997). *Web-based instruction*. Englewood Cliffs, NJ: Educational Technology Publications.

Knox, E. L. S. (2002). *The pedagogy of web site design.* ALN Magazine: A Publication of the Sloan Consortium. Retrieved November 12, 2003 from http://www.aln.org/publications/magazine/v1n2/knox.asp.

Lazonder, A. (2003). Principles for designing web searching instruction. *Education and Information Technologies,. 8, 2.*

Maskell, R. (2003).   Taking learning to the next level. *Military Training Technology: Online Edition.* Retrieved November 15, 2003, from http://www.mt2-kmi.com.

McAlister, M., Rivera, J., & Hallam, S. (2001). Twelve important questions to answer before you offer a web-based curriculum. *Online Journal of Distance Learning Administration, 4, 2.*

Montilva, J. A., Sandia, B., & Barrios, J. (2002). Developing instructional Web sites–a software engineering approach. *Education and Information Technologies, 7(3),* 201-224.

Moore, M. G. (1997). The study guide: Foundation of the course. Editorial note. *The American Journal of Distance Education, 11(2),* 1-2.

Nash, S. (2003). *Online course quality benchmarks.* Retrieved November 30, 2003, from http://intercom. virginia.edu/ SurveySuite/Surveys/Course_Benchmarks.

Nielsen, J. (1996). *Top ten Web design mistakes. Jakob Nielsen's alertbox.* Retrieved November 1, 2003, from http://www.useit.com/alertbox.

O'Donoghue, J., Jentz, A., Singh, G., & Molyneux, S. (2001). IT developments and changes in customer demand in higher education. *ALN Magazine*, 4, 1.

O'Sullivan, M. F. (1999). Worlds within which we teach: Issues for designing world wide web course material. *Technical Communication Quarterly, 8*(1), 61-72.

Paasonen, S. (2002). The woman question: Addressing women as internet users. In Domain errors! Cyberfeminist practices. *Autonomedia and SubRosa*, 89-108.

Palloff, R. M., & Pratt, K. (1999). *Building learning communities in cyberspace*. San Francisco: Jossey-Bass.

Ragan, L. C. (1999). Good teaching is good teaching: An emerging set of guiding principles and practices for the design and development of distance education. *Cause/Effect, 22*,1. Retrieved December 22, 2003, from http://www.educause.edu/ir/library/html/cem9915.html.

Reeves, T. (2002). A model of the effective dimensions of interactive learning on the World Wide Web. *Instructional Technology Resources, University of Georgia.* Retrieved November 10, 2003, from http://it.coe.uga/ ~treeves/WebPaper.pdf.

Roberson, T., & Klotz, J. (2002). How can instructors and administrators fill the missing link in online instruction? *Online Journal of Distance Learning Administration*, 5, 4.

Rosenberg, M. J. (2001). *E-learning: Strategies for delivering knowledge in the digital age.* New York: McGraw-Hill.

Schweizer, H. (1999). *Designing and teaching an online course.* Boston: Allyn & Bacon.

Sloan-C. (2002). *Effective practices.* Retrieved November 3, 2003, from http://www.aln.org.

University of Central Florida. (1999). *Best practices for authorship, design, and Web site management.* Retrieved November 1, 2003, from http://www.ucf.edu/webpolicy/reports/specreport-REV8text.htm

University of Tasmania. (2002). *Web publishing policy and guidelines.* Retrieved November 15, 2003, from http://www.utas.edu.au/webdev/docs/web_publishing_guidelines.pdf .

Wolfe, T. E. (1996). *Putting interaction into interactive television.* In Proceedings, 17th Annual Distance Learning Conference, University of Wisconsin, Madison, WI.

DISTANCE LEARNING FOR BUSINESS:

IS PERCEPTION REALITY?

John A. Rushing
Barry University

Jean N. Gordon
St. Thomas University

Richard Murphy
Nova Southeastern University

INRODUCTION

Market demands and organizational pressure have driven strong growth in delivery of business learning at a distance (Hayes, 2000; Murphy, 1999, April 5; Santosus, 1997). However, serious concerns have been raised about the quality of learning outcomes, particularly with respect to Web-based courses (Noble, 2001). In this article an embedded assessment process intended to address the quality concern is discussed. Next, a research study is described that utilized that process to compare learning outcomes in face-to-face and Web-delivered courses.

BACKGROUND

Harvard, Brown and M.I.T. have recently announced their decisions to board the business e-teaching bandwagon (Forelle, 2003, January 15). They join a rapidly expanding movement to deliver business teaching via the Web (Hayes, 2000). However, voices of concern about quality of learning outcomes are being heard from a variety of sources.

T.H.E. Journal reported upon the research of Jim DiPerna and Rob Volpe who reviewed more than 250 articles over a 10 year time period. They found only 12 articles that evaluated quality in Web-delivered courses and of these 11 were based solely on self-reported student perceptions—only one study directly assessed learning outcomes (Farrington & Bonack, 2001, May). Wall Street Journal reporter John D. McKinnon reported that professors at Florida Gulf Coast University, an institution "built as a testing ground for Internet-based instruction" expressed serious concerns and reservations regarding the effectiveness of distance learning (McKinnon, 1998, p. 14c). David Noble's thought provoking and chilling analysis has been cause for many progressive curriculum designers to pause and reflect upon the implications of Web delivery in the historical context of the correspondence course diploma mills of the past (Noble, 2001).

A great deal has been written about how to deliver Web learning, but less about assessing the quality of Web delivery (Sanders, 2001; Syrett, 1998). It is in this context that the authors decided to develop a process for assessment of learning outcomes in Web-delivered courses and to perform a test of that process.

THE CURRENT STUDY

Study Description

The purpose of the study was to test the assessment process and to measure the delivery of quality learning outcomes to students using a blended delivery mode (face-to-face and Web) as opposed to a strictly face-to-face traditional delivery mode. This study compared learning outcomes of three sample populations by comparing their means and variances. One population was a face-to-face Diversity in the Workplace sample, consisting of 55 students from two classes. Another population was a control group consisting of 32 students from one class. The third population was a Diversity in the Workplace sample that consisted of 37 students in two classes, which utilized Web delivery blended with face-to-face delivery, i.e., with half the classes delivered in person.

Two professors were involved in teaching the Administration classes. Each professor taught one face-to-face class and one Web class, i.e., four classes were taught at two separate locations by two different professors. This was done to control as many variables as possible so that any differences in learning outcomes could be ascribed to differences in delivery methods rather than differences in location, teacher etc. A separate fifth class was used as a control group. This class had been taught in a previous term by one of the professors involved in the study but prior to the initiation of the study. The control class was taught in the face-to-face delivery mode.

Process Development

The process began with an acceptance of the assumption that simply asking students their opinion about learning outcomes was not a satisfactory substitute for objective assessment of learning outcomes. Another assumption was that a single measure of learning was not sufficient. Some students will score better on short answer exams and some will score better on essay exams or term papers. Another consideration was standardization so that assessment could be conducted in different geographic locations because the school sampled had sites widely distributed over a large state. Finally, since the student population consisted of adult learners in an Administration program, it was decided to select a Junior level (300) class from the core curriculum. Figure 1 maps the process.

Figure 1
Assessment Process

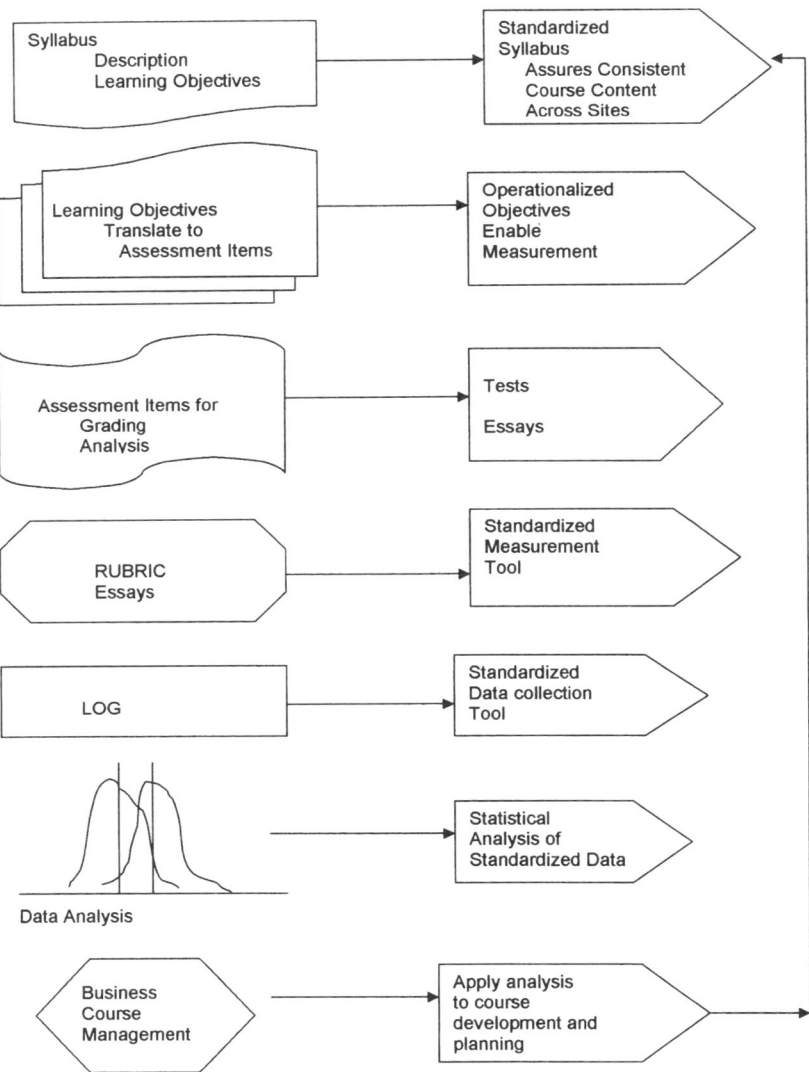

Learning Objectives

Learning objectives were clearly identified through a faculty focus group. These learning objectives were associated with levels of cognitive operations identified in Bloom's Taxonomy (Bloom et. al.,1956). This was desirable so that appropriate levels of learning matched levels that were required for upper level or lower level courses. For example, higher learning levels were required for Junior and Senior level courses.

As a result of the assumptions we selected an embedded assessment process. A faculty focus group developed a standardized course syllabus so each instructor would be using the same syllabus, text and support materials. This was done to eliminate as many confounding variables as possible from the process design. The syllabus and the process were evaluated by a faculty curriculum committee as a quality assurance method.

Operationalized Objectives

Next, the learning objectives were operationalized. This was done so that the learning outcomes could be objectively measured. For example, learning objective six stated: *Upon successful completion of the course the student should be able to analyze a diversity problem in an organization and develop a systematic solution to the problem applying both theory and practice in the solution (synthesis, analysis, evaluation and application).* The research team decided that this upper level learning would require more sophisticated measurement. Therefore basic knowledge or comprehension assessments such as multiple choice examinations or short answer tests were eliminated.

Ultimately an applied project consisting of a combination of written paper and oral defense emerged as logical operationalization. For the lower levels such as knowledge and comprehension the objectives were operationalized using statements that could be measured using short answer or multiple choice questions.

Assessment Items

Two assessment items were identified—final examinations and applied projects. To assure consistency the team decided to use a standard final exam drawn from the professors teaching the selected course; i.e., all students would take the identical exam. To assure uniformity in grading the applied project a grading rubric was developed and pre-tested (Godar & Knaus, 2002). The applied research projects consisted of an applied research paper (term paper) and an oral delivery to the class of the research outcomes described in the applied paper. Grading was facilitated using a standardized Rubric.

Grading Rubric

A grading rubric was used to assure consistent assessment of key operationalized learning outcomes from the course syllabus. Applied projects present a challenge in grading because there is not a "correct" answer. Thus both students and their professors have problems in evaluating the merits of the papers. Rubrics, which may be defined as scaling tools that provide descriptions for a continuum of performance levels, may be used to meet this challenge (Simon & Forgett-Giroux, 2001). Rubrics can help students assess the quality of their work before it is graded so they can perform self-evaluation and self-correction. For professors, the rubric provides a cross-check and significantly reduces "bounce-back" from student questioning their grades. In practice, rubrics tend to speed up the grading process for professors. (Godar & Knaus, 2002). A sample grading rubric appears in Table 1.

Table 1
Sample Grading Rubric

CRITERION/TRAIT	5	4	3	2	1
Written Communication – Organization Score:____	Writing is clearly organized. Each paragraph is clear and relates to others in a well-organized framework		Writing demonstrates sufficient organization with a clear thesis and supporting details.		Writing is rambling and unfocused. Major topic and supporting arguments are presented in a disorganized and unrelated way.
Written Communication – Language Use Score:____	Writing is excellent. Word usage, spelling, grammar, and punctuation are excellent.		Writing is sufficient. Adequate use of wording, grammar, and punctuation. Errors are minimal		Writing is poor. Significant deficiencies in word use, grammar, punctuation, and/or presentation.
References/citation system Score:____	All sources are cited correctly and thoroughly (in text and on reference page); APA citation system is used consistently and correctly.		All sources are cited, the majority cited correctly (in text and on reference page); APA citation system is used correctly for majority of citations.		Some sources are cited correctly (in text and on reference page); APA format is not used or used for a minority of citations. Or, no reference page is present.
Format/mechanics Score:____	Paper is at least 1500 words, double-spaced with 1" margins. Format enhances the clarity of the paper.		Paper is at least 1500 words, double-spaced. Format has limited effect on clarity of the paper.		Paper is not at least 1500 words, double-spaced. Format harms the clarity of the paper.

Critical thinking/problem solving Score:_____	Problem is clearly identified. Concepts, assumptions, inferences, and conclusions are clearly and thoroughly expressed. Analysis is logical and thorough.		Concepts, assumptions, inferences, and conclusions are expressed clearly in most cases but are not expressed thoroughly. Analysis is mostly logical but may be absent or flawed in some places.		Problem is not clearly identified. Concepts, assumptions, inferences, and conclusions are unclear, may be absent or flawed logic may be present. Analysis is minimal or absent or the logic used in argument may not be discerned. No Solution is presented.
Application of theories Score:_____	Culture theory is clearly identified in terms of the specified application to the solution of the diversity problem.		Culture theory is satisfactorily explained in terms of the specified application to solution of the problem.		Culture theory is poorly explained in terms of the specified application of the diversity problem.
Use of course material Score:_____	All relevant course material is used. Specific information from readings and lectures is incorporated into analysis and critique.		Majority of relevant course material is used. General information from readings and lectures is incorporated into analysis and critique.		Minimal course material is used. Information from readings and lectures is not incorporated into analysis and critique.

Model rubric developed by Karen Callaghan

Log

This standardized data collection tool was developed in another school of the university. It had proven useful in facilitating comparison of data across classes and schools. All scores are standardized on the basis of a five point scale that is applied in the grading rubrics. This allows history class averages to be compared with literature class averages as well as allowing inter-and intra-class comparisons. The log melds with the grading rubrics particularly effectively and to a significant degree facilitates the difficult process of comparing essay results.

Course Design and Management

The final component in the process is feedback of assessment results into the design and implementation of the course. For example, the main complaint voiced by student in the Web-delivered class was a feeling of isolation. Students in the Web-delivered class missed the interaction with the professor that other students typically experienced in the face-to-face classes. So the course designers suggested a re-design of some of the Web components to make greater use of "chat" features on the Blackboard system. They also suggested inclusion of some team activities that require interaction by the students. Although this was not a learning outcome issue, it was an important learning moment for the course developers.

An analysis of the pattern of missed questions on the final exam revealed that certain factual information from one key chapter was consistently missed across all groups. This suggests that instructors may want to devote more class time or more emphasis to these sections of the chapter. In contrast, we did not find a pattern of missed questions that was isolated to either the control class, the face-to-face classes or the Web-delivered classes. This is both comforting and a little surprising. It is comforting because it implies consistency across all classes. It is somewhat surprising because one might reasonably expect significant differences, at least between classes taught by different professors.

Process Application

Figure 2 graphically illustrates key components of the application of the process. Learning objectives from the standardized syllabus are operationalized into measurable assessment items. The grading rubric is used to measure the operationalized learning outcome.

Figure 2
Process Application

Learning Objectives (Example)

6.   Upon successful completion of the course the student should be able to analyze a diversity problem in an organization and develop a systematic solution to the problem applying both theory and practice in the solution. (synthesis, analysis, evaluation and application)

Assessment Item

       All students are required to prepare an applied paper for an organization of their choosing. The paper will identify a diversity problem and propose a solution. The solution must incorporate materials from the course including, but not limited to, the text and articles. The paper must be typed or computer printed and will contain appropriate documentation including at least three peer-reviewed articles. APA style will be used. The paper, which will be not less than 1500 words in length, will be turned in by Class Period Eight. The paper will be assessed using the Rubric on page 5.

CRITERION/TRAIT	5	4	3	2	1
Written Communication – Organization Score:_____	Writing is clearly organized. Each paragraph is clear and relates to others in a well-organized framework		Writing demonstrates sufficient organization with a clear thesis and supporting details.		Writing is rambling and unfocused. Major topic and supporting arguments are presented in a disorganized and unrelated way.
Written Communication – Language Use Score:_____	Writing is excellent. Word usage, spelling, grammar, and punctuation are excellent.		Writing is sufficient. Adequate use of wording, grammar, and punctuation. Errors are minimal		Writing is poor. Significant deficiencies in word use, grammar, punctuation, and/or presentation.
References/citation system Score:_____	All sources are cited correctly and thoroughly (in text and on reference page); APA citation system is used consistently and correctly.		All sources are cited, the majority cited correctly (in text and on reference page); APA citation system is used correctly for majority of citations.		Some sources are cited correctly (in text and on reference page); APA format is not used or used for a minority of citations. Or, no reference page is present.

ANALYSES AND RESULTS

Data Analysis

The focus of this process is assessment of learning outcomes across groups. Thus populations of interest are groups being taught using traditional face-to-face approaches and groups being taught using a Web approach. Data was collected using the standardized log so that useful comparisons of group learning outcomes could be made.

A useful way to describe a dimension of a population or sample is to measure the mean and standard deviation of the dimension. Likewise, a useful way of comparing two populations with respect to a dimension or variable of interest is to compare the means and standard deviations of the dimensions or variables of interest. One statistical methodology appropriate to this process is to compare the means and standard deviations (variances) using the two-tailed independent samples t-test for comparison of means and the Levene test of variances as a test of standard deviations. This type of analysis was selected for the study. SPSS version 8.0 software was used for the data analyses.

Results

Results of the data analyses are provide in Table 2.

Table 2
Learning Outcomes Data Analysis

Learning Outcomes on Applied Project (Blended vs. F2F)

	Descriptives			Levene		t-test	
Project	N	Mean	σ	F	Sig.	t	Sig.
F2F	55	16.3327	1.6246	2.653	.107	-1.131	.261
Blended	37	16.7862	2.2216				

Ho   Means are equal.   At α=.05, fail to reject the null hypothesis.

Learning Outcomes on Final Exam (Blended vs. F2F)

	Descriptives			Levene		t-test	
Exam	N	Mean	σ	F	Sig.	t	Sig.
F2F	55	17.6782	1.9314	.010	.921	1.393	.167
Blended	37	17.1378	1.66525				

Ho   Means are equal. At α=.05, fail to reject the null hypothesis.

Learning Outcomes on Applied Project (F2F vs. Control)

	Descriptives			Levene		t-test	
Project	N	Mean	σ	F	Sig.	t	Sig.
F2F	55	16.3327	1.6346	1.657	.201	-1.185	.239
Control	32	16.7188	1.1335				

Ho   Means are equal. At α=.05, fail to reject the null hypothesis.

Learning Outcomes on Final Exam (F2F vs. Control)

	Descriptives			Levene		t-test	
Exam	N	Mean	σ	F	Sig.	t	Sig.
F2F	55	17.6782	1.9314	.327	.569	2.925	**.004**
Control	32	16.5163	1.5026				

Ho   Means are equal.   At α=.05, **reject the null hypothesis.**

Stated briefly there were no significant differences between the control class, the face-to-face class and the blended class with respect to learning outcomes as measured by performance on applied research projects. There were no significant differences between the final exam outcomes of the face-to-face and blended classes; however, there was a small but statistically significant difference between the control group final exam outcomes and the face-to-face class final exam outcomes. This unexpected outcome could at least be partially explained by inferring migration of information across classes, which was facilitated by use of the same examination in all classes. Although the choice to use the same examination was rational analytically, particularly in light of the geographic separation of the classes, it may have ignored the realities of human behavior.

CONCLUSIONS AND RECOMMENDATIONS FOR FURTHER RESEARCH

The functionality of the assessment process was supported. Both Instructors and students felt that the assessments fairly portrayed the actual learning achieved in the courses. However, that does not mean generalizations from these results to other courses or other combinations of delivery format can automatically be made. It is possible that learning outcomes in the Administration classes were artifacts of the discipline or other factors. It is also possible that fully online courses will produce different learning outcomes than courses that still include some significant portion of face-to-face delivery. Additional studies are clearly called for.

First, this study should be repeated with respect to the Diversity in the Workplace course to confirm the findings. Second, an expanded study should be conducted using different courses from a variety of disciplines to confirm that results are not an artifact of a particular course or discipline.

In addition, the next step in the study will require improved controls for the final examination, possibly including randomly drawn tests from a validated bank of test questions, which was unavailable in this study.. Colleagues have also suggested that there should be a double blind reading of the applied project papers.

Results may, in part, be explained by the element of self-selection in the populations, as students were not randomly assigned to classes. Due to student input, in the end nearly three quarters of the students elected to take the face to face class (Weber & Lennon, 2001)

Another element that will require measurement is student satisfaction. Student evaluations, either ones presently used to evaluate faculty, or a modification of such surveys, could be constructively included in the next study.

The next step in this research will be to feedback initial results and seek approval from the curriculum committee to evaluate learning outcomes for a fully on-line course compared to a face-to-face course using the same design and process described above for the face-to-face and blended delivery courses. This conservative approach is a reflection of serious concerns among faculty and administration with respect to the quality of learning outcomes.

REFERENCES

Bloom, B. S., Englehart, M. D., Furts, F. J., Hill, W. H.& Krathwohl, D. R. (1956). *Taxonomy of educational objectives: Cognitive domain.* New York: McKay.

Farrington, G., & Bonack, S. (2001, May). Sink or swim: Higher education on line: How do we know what works— and what doesn't? *T.H.E. Journal*, 70-76.

Forelle, C. (2003, January 15). Elite colleges finally embrace online degree courses. *Wall Street Journal*, B1.

Godar, S. H., & Knaus, E. J. (2002). Developing rubrics for global marketing cases. *Proceedings of the Academy of International Business*, 114-116.

Hayes, H. (2000). Vendors see virtual classroom as real-time business. *Washington Technology, 14*(3), 22-36.

McKinnon, J. D. (1998, September 6). Online courses demand more of professors. *The Tallahassee Democrat*, p. 14c.

Murphy, K. (1999, April 5). Welcome to the world of MBA.com. *Business Week*, p. 120.

Noble, D. F. (2001). *Digital diploma mills: The automation of higher education*. New York: Monthly Review Press.

Sanders, W. B. (2001). *Creating learning-centered courses for the World Wide Web*. Boston: Allyn and Bacon.

Santosus, M. (1997). Degrees of change. *CIO* , 10(15), 78-86.

Simon, M., & Forgett-Giroux, R. (2001). A rubric for scoring postsecondary academic skills. *Practical Assessment, Research and Evaluation, 7*(18).

Syrett, M. (1998). Going the distance. *Director*, 51(12), 76.

Weber, M, & Lennon, R (2001). *A comparison between a Web-based course delivery system with a traditional course delivery system*. Unpublished research study.

ACCOMMODATING LEARNING STYLES

THROUGH HYPERMEDIA-ENHANCED

INSTRUCTION

Malgorzata S. Zywno
Ryerson University

INTRODUCTION

Hypermedia and Learner Achievement

Technology is changing our understanding of the nature of learning. The implications for education are profound, from infrastructure to research methodologies, faculty attitudes, teaching paradigms and classroom practice. There has been an exponential growth of publications on hypermedia (an outgrowth of hypertext, providing a non-linear, associative linking of text, graphics, video, and sounds). Yet the literature review reveals a dearth of empirical studies on its effects on learning in the context of a real curriculum.

This can be in part traced to the famous "Media vs. Method" debate in which Clark (1994) tirelessly argued against media comparison studies. Despite contrary arguments that in the present era of constructivism and distributed cognition learning has been redefined with media providing support for instruction that would not have been otherwise possible (Jonassen, 2000; Kozma, 1994; 2000; Winn, 2002), many researchers have accepted Clark's thesis that media do not contribute to increased learning (Russell, 1999; Surry & Ensminger, 2001).

A divide grew between learning research and media development, proceeding without much input from the former (Hokanson, 2001), despite calls to conduct more classroom-based action research to narrow that gap (Driscoll & Dick, 1999). Existing meta-analyses on the effectiveness of computer-or hypermedia-assisted learning (Ayersman, 1996; Dillon & Gabbard, 1998; Liao, 1999) often have conflicting conclusions. Few of the reported studies meet scientific requirements for selection, manipulation and control of potential mediating variables, as researchers face many difficulties in trying to conduct controlled studies in university settings where threats to validity and reliability are often beyond their influence (Reeves, 2000). Shortages of empirical research are particularly dire in engineering education (Kadiyala & Crynes, 2000). Researchers are often unaware of the vast body of research available outside their field and many studies suffer from poor controls (Wankat et al., 2002).

Faculty Attitudes and Use of Technology

Inconsistent results of studies on hypermedia efficacy underscore the fact that the educational technology itself does not produce learning; what matters is how it is used. The evidence is accumulating that hypermedia is most effective in the context of student-centered education, where it has to be grounded firmly in curriculum goals and incorporated into the instructional process (Bransford, Brophy & Williams, 2000; Catalano & Catalano, 1999; Smith & Waller, 1997).

Yet the culture of engineering departments does not promote educational development of faculty (Stice et al., 2000; Wankat et al., 2002). Teaching is systemically undervalued across the whole university system, where one can teach based on field expertise alone and without completing any educational training (Bruffee, 1999; Froyd,

2002). Low priority for the scholarship of teaching in hiring and promotion policies, lack of training and force of habits result in instructor-centered teaching practices that are not conductive to independent study and critical thinking skills. Professors often follow familiar patterns, teaching in a style correlated with their personality traits, or aligned with what they were exposed to in college (Bruffee, 1999; Fuller, Norby & Pierce, 2000).

Research on Learning Styles

Chickering and Gamson (1991) wrote in their meta-analysis of 50 years of research that good practice respects diverse talents and ways of learning, and students need opportunities to learn in ways that work for them. There is increasing recognition that a "chalk & talk" lecture does not accommodate all types of learners, and the shift toward student-centered learning fuels interest in learning styles.

Learning style is defined as a manner in which learners consistently respond to and process information in a learning environment, and is thought to be an individual characteristic that does not change over time. Different models have been developed, with corresponding psychometric instruments. Correlation between learning styles and learning outcomes is not well defined. In an extensive literature review, Stahl (1999) found no detectable improvement from attempts to create a teaching style to match learning styles. Attempts to use learning styles as a tool to predict student success and retention also failed (Van Zwanenberg, Wilkinson & Anderson, 2000).

Dillon and Gabbard (1998), in their extensive review of quantitative research on hypermedia as an educational technology speculate that the current array of learning style models was not capable of capturing nuances of that correlation on a statistically significant level. More likely, this is so because psychometric tools only indicate possibility, not probability, of certain results. All learners follow their preferences at some times, and act against them at other times, depending on circumstances. Thus, learning styles are not invariant predictors of behavior, and should not be used to predict the likelihood of success or failure (Felder & Spurlin, 2003). The point of identifying them is not to label students and modify instruction to fit their labels. A strong case can be made against such instruction, as to function effectively as professionals, students will need skills associated with different learning style dimensions, and a balanced teaching style that accommodates a broad spectrum of tasks suitable for different preferences can help them achieve their learning objectives more efficiently (Felder, 1996, December; Saracho, 1998). This supports cognitive flexibility theory (Jacobson & Spiro, 1995) and teaching "around the cycle," promoted to enhance learning (Chickering & Gamson, 1991; Cowan, 1998; Felder, 1996, December; Kolb, 1984).

On the other hand, teaching students in a manner almost entirely mismatched with their preferences may cause them sufficient discomfort leading to lower achievement, dissatisfaction and increased dropout rates (Felder & Silverman, 1988; Smith & Waller, 1997, Wankat et al., 2002). Yet, while the literature suggests that traditional instruction does not support the learning styles of the majority of engineering students, it is still prevalent in engineering departments (Catalano & Catalano, 1999; Wankat et al., 2002).

Felder Learning Model

Felder and Silverman (1988) developed a learning model that focuses specifically on aspects of learning styles of engineering students. Its psychometric instrument, the Index of Learning Styles (Felder & Soloman, 2001), has four dimensions:

- Processing (Active vs. Reflective)

- Perception (Sensing vs. Intuitive)

- Input (Visual vs. Verbal)

- Understanding (Sequential vs. Global).

The study described in this paper contributed to the ongoing validation work on the Index of Learning Styles through the analyses of test-retest reliability, factor structure, internal reliability, total item correlation, inter-scale correlation and construct validity of the available responses (Zywno, 2003a).

Hypermedia and Learning Styles

Because of multi-modal attributes involved, it has been suggested that hypermedia may be effective in accommodating a broader range of learning style preferences (Ayersman, 1996; Dillon & Gabbard, 1998). This hypothesis was explored in the study, using the Felder model to assemble a students' learning preferences profile and to provide an insight into how teaching strategies can be modified to broaden their appeal. Equally importantly, its dimensions were directly related to the instructional design.

THE STUDY

The study was conducted in a Control Systems course (ELE639) in an undergraduate program in Electrical and Computer Engineering at Ryerson University in Toronto. In 1999, hypermedia and online WebCT support were introduced with the goal to enhance active learning and visualization, lessen the reliance on lecturing, increase participation and encourage reflection, all necessary ingredients of learning (Cowan, 1998).

The 1999 pilot study showed improved achievement on common exams, and a rigorous comparison study of technology-assisted and conventional learning environments followed in 2000. As significant improvements in achievement were again observed, the comparison study was discontinued as incompatible with the objective of increased learning. Since 2001, the focus shifted to interactions with hypermedia among different types of learners, discussion of threats to study validity and attitudinal domain. A survey of faculty teaching strategies provided a context for the findings.

In 2002, online quizzes with immediate feedback were introduced, as was the "one minute paper". The students wrote about the "muddiest point" and the most salient point of the lecture as they understood it. The next class would begin with the discussion of topics related to the feedback. More interaction was encouraged through the use of "buzz groups" and "think-pair-share" activities. As the class size increased, the group size increased as well, from three to six students, and self-and peer-evaluations and group mentoring were introduced to improve engagement and motivation.

In 2003, with the enrollment of 176, student engagement became more challenging. The introduction of an Internet research project helped ameliorate that somewhat. A voluntary competition was introduced. Student teams were invited to enter a bidding process to make formal presentations for the whole class. Twelve teams submitted written proposals, which were then adjudicated with the input from students and teaching assistants. The four winning teams consulted with the instructor throughout the semester. All students were involved in evaluations of technical content and communication skills of presenters. Small bonus marks were assigned based on the class input. The exercise engaged 40% of the class (N=72) in the proposals, and the whole class in adjudicating the competition. High levels of engagement, enthusiasm and creativity were observed throughout the process.

STUDY FINDINGS

Context for the Study: Instructional Strategies and Learning Styles

Between 2000 and 2002, 338 students (92% return rate) completed the Index of Learning Styles questionnaire. The students were predominantly Active, Sensing, Visual and Sequential learners. This is consistent with profiles of engineering students in several countries (Felder & Spurlin, 2003; Van Zwanenberg et al., 2000). In 2002, a survey of learning styles and teaching strategies of engineering faculty (N=48, 27% return rate) was conducted (Zywno, 2003b). The comparison revealed a mismatch between the learning styles of engineering students and faculty, as shown in Table 1. More importantly, the faculty survey showed predominance of conventional, lecture-based teaching strategies, which accommodated only a small segment of student learning preferences. Low participation in educational activities and low use of innovative instructional methods and instructional technologies were also reported. This trend, particularly visible among younger faculty, is also consistent with the literature.

Table 1
Differences in Distributions of Modalities
Between Students and Faculty

	N	Ref.	Act.	Int.	Sen.	Verb.	Vis.	Glo.	Seq.
Faculty	48	**62.5%**	37.5%	**58.3%**	41.7%	6.2%	**93.8%**	**64.6%**	35.4%
Students	338	39.1%	**60.9%**	35.2%	**64.8%**	11.8%	**88.2%**	37.3%	**62.7%**
Chi-Square		χ^2=11.087, df=1, p=0.001 **		χ^2=11.254, df=1, p=0.001 **		χ^2=1.435, df=1, p=0.231		χ^2=15.306, df=1, p=0.0005***	

The survey results help in interpretation of the data showing that the students whose learning styles were not consistent with that instructional style were more likely to be over-represented in the group labeled as underachieving prior to the course in the study.

Prior academic achievement score PAA was based on the students' Term Grade Point Average (six courses prior to ELE639). Cumulative Grade Point Average score CGPA (all previous courses) and the PRG score based on a grade in a pre-requisite course were also tracked. All three scores were reflective of the conventional learning environment. To assess different levels of prior achievement, two equal-size populations of students were defined using the median PAA score, and referred to as "previously above the median" PAM, and "previously below the median" PBM.

If the learning style preferences had no effect on the achievement, it could be expected that for each style 50% of its members would be performing below the median, while the other 50% would be performing above the median. However, when student learning styles were correlated with their PAA, CGPA and PRG scores, Active,

Sensing, Visual and Global learners were disproportionately over-represented in the below the median, or underachieving, group. Differences in the style distributions between above the median and below the median groups were statistically significant.

Negative correlation was found between the Reflective and Intuitive scores of the faculty and their reported use of student-centered strategies. This is consistent with the model and can be interpreted as the tendency to choose individual strategies discouraging engagement and cooperation, and the lack of need for concrete information. The learning preferences of the faculty in the survey (Reflective and Inductive) are thus reflected in their choices of instructional strategies.

The negative correlation between the Visual score and the use of simulations and multimedia seems at first counterintuitive to the patterns expected of Visual learners, as does the lack of correlation between the Global score and the reported (low) use of "big picture" overview strategies. However, since holistic, interdisciplinary teaching that fosters creativity and problem-solving skills, and the use of instructional technology both require a significant preparation effort, one can surmise that the decision to implement them would be more affected by the pedagogical philosophy, time available and priority assigned to teaching than by a mere learning preference.

Low priority of teaching evident in the survey is consistent with the literature. It also explains a paradox of predominantly Visual and Global faculty favoring "chalk & talk", verbal, deductive and sequential lecturing styles, the last two reinforcing in the students qualities that do not serve engineering professionals well.

Student Achievement in Technology-rich Environment: A Comparison Study

In 1999 and 2000, one group of ELE639 students was instructed using hypermedia, and the other received conventional lectures. In 2001, both groups received hypermedia-enhanced instruction, but from two different instructors. Academic achievement was operationalized by course grades CG. Group differences in CG represented a measure of the effectiveness of the treatment. PAA score was used as a covariate in the ANCOVA analysis. With the quasi-experimental design, a probabilistic near-equivalency of the two groups was shown based on the PAA scores and demographic profiles (Zywno, 2002a).

The covariate was also used to compute expected course grades and residuals (a difference between the actual scores and the expected scores based on the PAA variance). The residual mean in a cohort is always zero, but they can identify groups performing better or worse than expected. Thus while the CG scores indicated academic performance in the course, its residuals provided an additional measure of performance improvement.

Table 2 shows group differences in CG and its residuals. As is customary for the F-ratio statistic from ANCOVA, the group means were adjusted for the covariate to allow a more meaningful interpretation of the results. The group differences were also captured using a meta-analytic approach (Glass, 1982), with the effect size ES defined as a difference between the means of two groups, divided by the pooled standard deviation. Group differences were statistically significant in 1999 and 2000, with the hypermedia-instructed groups performing better in the course (as well as in the common exam), but negligible in 2001 when both groups receiving hypermedia instruction.

Table 2
Group Differences in Course Grades,
Adjusted for PAA, in %

	1999		2000		2001	
	HYPER	CONV	HYPER	CONV	HYPER	HYPER
Number of students	57	37	49	45	66	62
Pooled Mean	78.44		66.06		75.37	
Group Mean	80.67	75.02	69.17	62.68	75.23	75.53
Residuals	2.188	-3.370	3.089	-3.363	-0.146	0.156
Pooled St. Deviation	8.289		9.112		6.512	
ANCOVA Statistic	F=11.287, df=1,91 p=0.001***		F=13.257, df=1,91 p=0.0004***		F=0.068, df=1,125 p=0.794	
Effect Size ES	0.68		0.71		-0.05	

*** Significant at .001 level (2 tailed)

In order to reject alternative explanations for group differences, a detailed analysis of several threats to the internal validity of the study was conducted (Zywno, 2002b). Selection bias, novelty factor, differences in instructional design and social threats (diffusion of treatment and resentful demoralization) were discussed and rejected. The impact of instructor differences, suggested in the literature (Dillon & Gabbard, 1998; Weller, 1996) was explored in detail. Two three-hour experiments were conducted in 2001, where the two instructors switched between conventional and technology-enabled presentations. Hypermedia-instructed group had significantly better results both times, regardless of the instructor. As Table 3 shows, no significant group differences were found when both instructors used conventional lectures prior to 1999, or active, technology-enabled learning techniques since 2001. This allowed for the instructor differences to be rejected as the possible threat to the study validity.

Table 3
Effect Sizes for Group Differences
in Course Grade CG (1996-2001)

'96	'97	'98	'99	'00	'01	'01a	'01b
A-c	A-c	B-c	A-h	A-h	A-h	A-h	A-c
C-c	B-c	C-c	C-c	B-c	B-h	B-c	B-h
ES=0.03	ES=-0.05	ES=-0.18	ES=0.68	ES=0.71	ES=-0.05	ES=0.91	ES=0.54

A,B,C - Instructors; h, c - Instructional Media; '01a, '01b - Switched Replications Test 1 and Test 2

Learning Styles and Student Achievement
in Technology-rich Environment

To assess different levels of achievement in ELE639, "above the median" AM and "below the median" BM groups were defined using the median value of CG. It was hypothesized that the use of instructional technology in the classroom and of Web support outside of it would significantly widen the range of supported learning styles. Indeed, as Figure 1 shows (2000-2002 data) differences in distributions of the learning styles in AM-BM groups were greatly moderated when compared with the distributions in PAM-PBM groups. In fact, unlike in the latter, the differences in style distributions between the AM and BM groups were no longer statistically significant.

Figure 1
Distributions of Modalities
between BM-AM Groups in PAA and CG

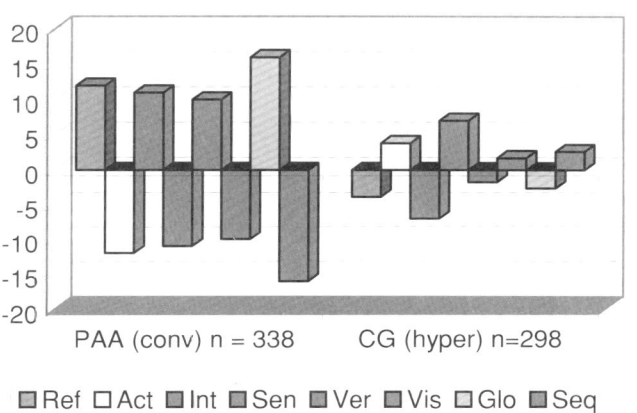

Chi-Square Residuals

□ Ref □ Act ■ Int ■ Sen ■ Ver ■ Vis □ Glo ■ Seq

The redistribution of learning styles helps explain a phenomenon of more rapid gains in technology-rich environment observed among the PBM students. There was a significant reduction of the differences between average achievement of PAM and PBM students in ELE639 (their CG score), as compared with their PAA score. While the effect sizes for the PAM-PBM differences in the PAA scores were consistently in the range of 1.61 to 1.65, the effect sizes for the difference in the CG scores between those two groups were reduced by more than 50%, to between 0.65 and 0.76. This effect was consistent across all learning style modalities, as shown in Figure 2 (2001 and 2002 data).

Figure 2
PAM-PBM Differences
for Different Learning Styles

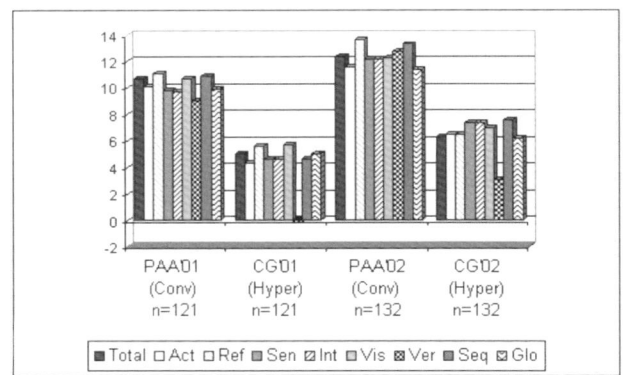

While their higher achieving peers were still getting better marks, the PBM students were able to significantly reduce the gap separating them from the PAM group. Their relatively more rapid improvement is consistent with the literature. Underachieving students typically have less-developed learning strategies and, according to the Cognitive Load Theory (Sweller, 2002) their cognitive load in processing information in the working memory is high. Better accommodation of all learning styles in the technology-rich environment through visualization and active learning benefits such students, many of whom had learning styles consistently not supported by the conventional teaching.

Another consequence of this beneficial effect was the increased "upward mobility" of the PBM students. Table 4 shows that in the conventional learning environments operationalized by the CGPA and PRG scores, as well as by the CG score prior to the 1999 introduction of instructional technology, approximately 80% of PBM students still performed at the below the-median level. However, after 1999, on average only 60% of

PBM students remained in the BM category of the CG score, while 40% moved up to the AM category. Thus, the technology-enriched environment made the statement "once underachiever, always underachiever" much less applicable.

Table 4
BM-AM Distributions in CGPA,
PRG and CG, w.r.t. PBM-PAM.

	CGPA Conventional		PRG Conventional		CG Conventional		CG Hypermedia	
	BM	AM	BM	AM	BM	AM	BM	AM
PBM '96	*	*	86%	14%	77%	23%	-	-
PAM '96	*	*	14%	86%	23%	77%	-	-
PBM '97	*	*	74%	26%	65%	35%	-	-
PAM '97	*	*	26%	74%	35%	65%	-	-
PBM '98	85%	15%	82%	18%	80%	20%	-	-
PAM '98	15%	85%	18%	82%	20%	80%	-	-
PBM '99	85%	15%	79%	21%	90%	10%	65%	35%
PAM '99	15%	85%	21%	79%	50%	50%	10%	90%
PBM '00	81%	19%	70%	30%	90%	10%	48%	52%
PAM '00	19%	81%	30%	70%	40%	60%	27%	72%
PBM '01	73%	27%	72%	28%	-	-	64%	36%
PAM '01	27%	73%	28%	72%	-	-	36%	64%
PBM '02	88%	12%	74%	26%	-	-	66%	34%
PAM '02	12%	88%	26%	74%	-	-	34%	66%
PBM Overall	**82%**	**18%**	**76%**	**24%**	**77%**	**23%**	**63%**	**37%**
PAM Overall	**18%**	**82%**	**24%**	**76%**	**30%**	**70%**	**30%**	**70%**

Student Satisfaction
with Technology-rich Environment

Student satisfaction with the instruction, Web access patterns and their correlation with the learning styles were also analyzed. Between 1999 and 2002, an exit survey was conducted among the ELE639 students (N=255, 75% return rate). Students overwhelmingly (87%) expressed their preference for the hypermedia-enhanced learning-teaching environment. Among the PBM students the approval rates were even higher (90%). These results are consistent with the literature (Angulo & Bruce, 1999; Kadiyala & Crynes, 2000). The preference was uniform across all modalities, as shown in Figure 3, ranging from 96.1% (Intuitive) to 79% (Verbal), with 91.3% average.

Figure 3
Learning Styles—Preference for
Technology-Enhanced Environment

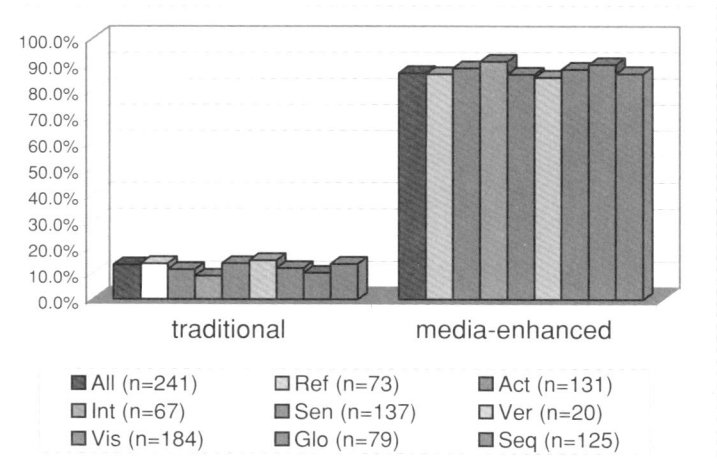

Figure 4 illustrates student satisfaction with the different components of the course, as the percentage of a possible maximum score. There were no significant differences between PBM and PAM students in any of the four years of the exit survey, or overall, in satisfaction with the lectures, Web support or with the course in general. A slight drop-off coincides with increases in the class size.

Figure 4
Course Satisfaction Scores from Exit Survey

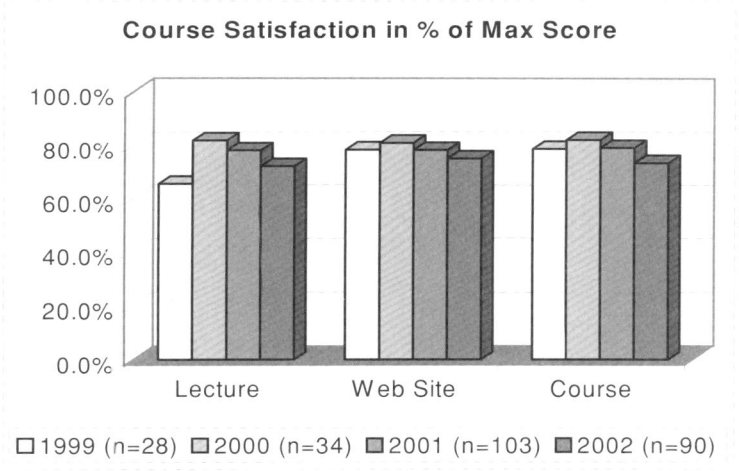

Figure 5 shows the mean satisfaction scores, as computed for the different learning style modalities. No significant differences were observed, with the scores uniformly high, with mean values ranging from 76.5% to 77.6%, except for the Verbal learners (72%). However, the sample of exit surveys corresponding to Verbal learners was also the smallest, with only 22 individuals over 4 years. Positive correlation was found between the Visual scores and the use of multimedia components and computer simulations, and between the Active scores and Bulletin

Board communications. Both are consistent with the Felder Model, which asserts the appeal of multimedia to Visual learners and of interactivity and collaboration to Active learners.

Figure 5
Learning Styles—Course Satisfaction Scores

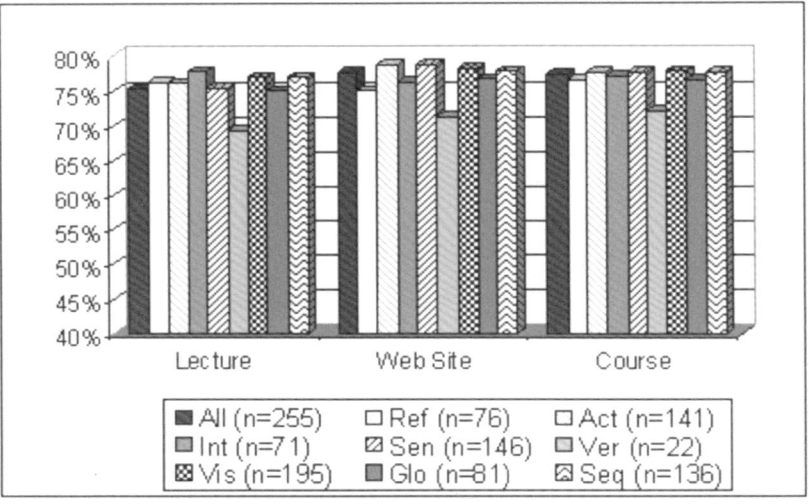

Longitudinal Effects

Over time, learning outcomes in the course were affected by educational technology in direct and indirect ways. The direct effects included the instructional media and Web support. The indirect effects included the impact of more active, collaborative strategies, made possible by the use of technology that freed class time for "value-added" activities (more interaction, mentoring, independent research). Figure 6 shows the trend over time in the examination grades. The first marked increase coincides with an introduction of hands-on experimentation in 1997, followed by Web-based lab tutorials in 1998. In 1999, following the introduction of the WebCT online support and educational technology, the grades improved both in the experimental and in the control group, which is most likely due to the diffusion of treatment effect. Yet group differences in 1999 and in 2000 were still statistically significant. Further slight increases occurred in 2002 and in 2003 despite the significant increases in the class size, and coincided with the introduction of online quizzes and group activities in 2002, followed by class presentations in 2003.

Figure 6
ELE639 Exam Scores over Time (1996-2003)

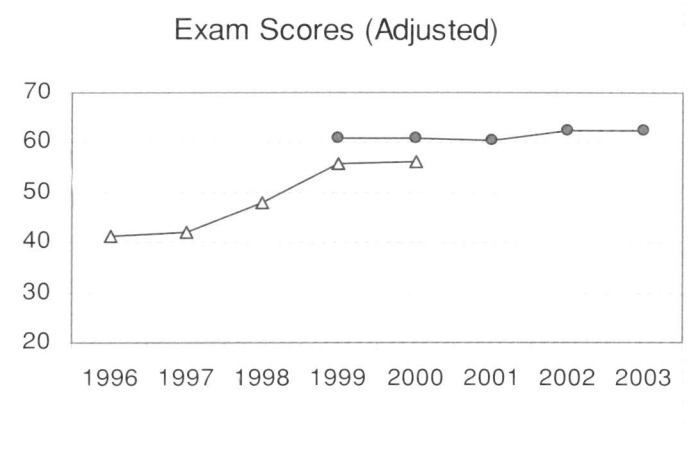

SUMMARY AND CONCLUSIONS

This study contributed to the state of existing research on the impact of technology on learning where few empirical investigations are conducted in authentic settings, particularly in engineering education. In addition, it offered significant support to the construct validity of the Felder Model of Learning Styles, and to the reliability analysis of its psychometric instrument, Index of Learning Styles.

The research showed that a technology-rich blended, or "hybrid" environment (in and outside of classroom) when implemented within a learner-centered framework, resulted in a significantly improved academic achievement, as compared with traditional instruction. Students reported preference for the hypermedia-enhanced learning and teaching environment, and a high level of satisfaction with it.

Effective scaffolding was provided for all students, but particularly for those previously labeled as underachieving, who disproportionately had learning styles that were not supported by the traditional instruction. They were able to develop more effective learning strategies, and gained rapidly. Not only was the achievement gap between them and their previously higher-achieving peers reduced, differences in distributions of learning styles between these two populations were significantly reduced as well.

While educational technology is often seen as a panacea for problems in education, it cannot alone equitably replace human interactions that contribute to learning. It is quite telling that in the exit surveys, over 75% of students consistently indicated their preference for technology to supplement, and not replace, interactions with their instructors and peers. The literature suggests that technology is most effective within the learner-centered pedagogical paradigm, when thoughtfully integrated into the instructional design. The study supports this point of view and confirms that pedagogical considerations should precede any discussion of how technology can enhance learning.

REFERENCES

Angulo, A. J., & Bruce, M. (1999). Student perceptions of supplemental web-based instruction. *Innovative Higher Education, 24*,105-125.

Ayersman, D. J. (1996). Reviewing the research on hypermedia-based learning. *Journal of Research on Computing in Education, 28*(4), 500-525.

Bransford, J., Brophy, S. & Williams, S. (2000). When computer technologies meet the learning sciences: issues and opportunities. *Journal of Applied Developmental Psychology, 21*(1), 59-84.

Bruffee, K. A. (1999). *Collaborative learning: Higher education, interdependence, and the authority of knowledge* (2nd ed.). Baltimore, MD: Johns Hopkins University Press.

Catalano, G. D. & Catalano, K. C. (1999). Transformation: From teacher-centered to student-centered engineering education. *Journal of Engineering Education, 88*(1), 59-64.

Chickering, A. W. & Gamson, Z. F. (1991). Applying the seven principles for good practice in undergraduate education. In A.W. Chickering. & Z. F. Gamson (Eds), *New directions for teaching and learning, 47.* San Francisco: Jossey-Bass.

Clark, R. E. (1994). Media will never influence learning. *Educational Technology Research and Development, 42* (2), 21-29.

Cowan, J. (1998). *On becoming an innovative university teacher.* Buckingham, UK: Society for Research into Higher Education and Open University Press.

Dillon, A. & Gabbard, R. (1998). Hypermedia as an educational technology: A review of the quantitative research literature on learner comprehension, control and style. *Review of Educational Research, 68*(3), 322-349.

Driscoll, M. P. & Dick, W. (1999). New research paradigms in instructional technology: An inquiry. *Educational Technology Research and Development, 47* (2), 7-18.

Felder, R. M. (1996, December). *Matters of style.* ASEE Prism Magazine, 18-23. Retrieved November, 2003 from http://www2.ncsu.edu/unity/lockers/users/f/felder/public/Papers/LS-Prism.htm

Felder, R. M. & Silverman, L. K. (1988). Learning and teaching styles in engineering education. *Journal of Engineering Education, 78*(7), 674-681.

Felder, R. M. & Soloman, B. A. (2001). *Index of Learning Styles questionnaire, North Carolina State University.* Retrieved November, 2003 from http://www2.ncsu.edu/unity/lockers/users/f/felder/public/ILSdir/ILS-a.htm

Felder, R. M. & Spurlin, J. (2003). *Psychometric analysis of the Index of Learning Styles,* North Carolina State University. Raleigh, North Carolina: unpublished.

Froyd, J. (2002). Model for inquiry and reflection about learning and teaching. In: W. Aung, P. Hicks, L. Scavard, V. Roubicek, V. Wei & C. H. Wei (Eds.), *Engineering education and research - 2001: A chronicle of worldwide innovations* (pp. 169-178). Arlington, VA: Ineer and Begell House.

Fuller, D., Norby, R. F. & Pearce, K (2000). Internet teaching by style: Profiling the on-line professor. *Educational Technology and Society, 3*(2). Retrieved November, 2003 from http://ifets.ieee.org/periodical/vol_2_2000/pearce.html.

Glass, G. V. (1982). Meta-analysis: An approach to the synthesis of research results. *Journal of Research in Science Teaching, 19*(2), 93-112.

Hokanson, B. (2001). Silk and silicon: Technology paradigms and education? *Educational Technology, 41*(3), 42-46.

Jacobson, M. J. & Spiro, R. J. (1995). Hypertext learning environments, cognitive flexibility and the transfer of complex knowledge: an empirical investigation. *Journal of Educational Computing Research, 12*(4), 301-333.

Jonassen, D. H. (2000). Transforming learning with technology: Beyond modernism and post-modernism or whoever controls the technology creates the reality. *Educational Technology, 50*(2), 21-25.

Kadiyala, M. & Crynes, B. L. (2000). A review of literature on effectiveness of use of information technology in education. *Journal of Engineering Education, 89*(2), 177-184.

Kolb, D.A. (1984). *Experiential learning: Experience as the source of learning and development.* Englewood Cliffs, NJ: Prentice Hall.

Kozma, R. B. (1994). Will media influence learning? Reframing the debate. *Educational Technology Research and Development, 42*(2), 7-19.

Kozma, R. B. (2000). Reflections on the state of educational technology research and development. *Educational Technology Research and Development, 48* (1), 5-15.

Liao, Y. C. (1999). Effects of hypermedia on students' achievement: A meta-analysis. *Journal of Educational Multimedia and Hypermedia, 8*(3), 255-277.

Reeves, T. C. (2000). *Enhancing the worth of instructional technology research through "Design Experiments" and other development research strategies.* Annual Meeting of the American Educational Research Association, New Orleans, LA. Retrieved November, 2003 from http://itech1.coe.uga.edu/~treeves/AERA2000Reeves.pdf.

Russell, T. L. (1999). *The "No Significant Difference" phenomenon.* Retrieved November, 2003 from http://cuda.teleeducation.nb.ca/nosignificantdifference.

Saracho, O. N. (1998). Research directions for cognitive style and education. *International Journal of Educational Research, 29,* 287-290.

Smith, K. A. & Waller, A. A. (1997). Afterward: New paradigms for college teaching. In W. Campbell & K. A. Smith. (Eds), *New paradigms for college teaching.* Edina, MN: Interactions Book.

Stahl, S. (1999, Fall). Different strokes for different folks? A critique of learning styles. *American Educator,* 27-31.

Stice, J. E., Felder, R. M., Woods, D. R. & Rugarcia, A. (2000). The future of engineering education IV: Learning how to teach. *Chemical Engineering Education, 34*(2), 118-127. Retrieved November, 2003 from http://www2.ncsu.edu/unity/lockers/users/f/felder/public/Papers/Quartet4.pdf

Surry, D. W. & Ensminger, D. (2001). What's wrong with media comparison studies? *Educational Technology, 41* (4), 32-35.

Sweller, J. (2002). *Visualization and instructional design.* Proceedings of the International Workshop on Dynamic Visualizations and Learning, 1501-1510, Knowledge Media Research Center (KMRC) Tübingen, Germany. Retrieved November, 2003 from http://www.iwm-kmrc.de/workshops/visualization/sweller.pdf

Van Zwanenberg, N., Wilkinson, L. J., & Anderson, A. (2000). Felder and Silverman's Index of Learning Styles and Honey and Mumford's Learning Styles questionnaire: How do they compare and do they predict academic performance? *Educational Psychology, 20*(3), 365-381.

Wankat, P. C., Felder, R. M., Smith, K. A., & Oreovicz, F. S. (2002). The scholarship of teaching and learning engineering. In M. T. Huber & S. Morreale (Eds.), *Disciplinary styles in the scholarship of teaching and learning: Exploring the common ground.* Washington, D. C.: AAHE/Carnegie Foundation for the Advancement of Teaching. Retrieved December, 2003, from http://www.ncsu.edu/felder-public/Papers/Scholarship_chapter.pdf.

Weller, H. G. (1996). Assessing the impact of computer-based learning in science. *Journal of Research on Computing in Education, 28*(4), 461-485.

Winn, W. (2002). Current trends in educational technology research: The study of learning environments. *Educational Psychology Review, 14*(3), 331-351.

Zywno, M. S. (2002a). *Instructional technology, learning styles and academic achievement.* Proceedings of the 2002 ASEE Annual Conference and Exposition, Montreal, Quebec.

Zywno, M. S. (2002b). *Threats to validity in a study of the effects of hypermedia instruction on learning outcomes— a switched replications experiment.* Proceedings of the 2002 ASEE Annual Conference and Exposition, Montreal, Quebec.

Zywno, M. S. (2003a). *A contribution to validation of score meaning for Felder-Soloman's Index of Learning Styles.* Proceedings of the 2003 ASEE Annual Conference and Exposition, Nashville, TN.

Zywno, M. S. (2003b), *Engineering faculty teaching styles and attitudes toward student-centered and technology-enabled teaching strategies.* Proceedings of the 2003 ASEE Annual Conference and Exposition, Nashville, TN.

CONTRIBUTORS

Phyllis D. Barham
Senior Lecturer, Nursing
Old Dominion University
E-mail: pbarham@odu.edu

Gerald D. Baumgardner
Associate Professor, Management
Pennsylvania College of Technology
E-mail: pbaumgar@pct.edu

Irene J. Caswell
Assistant Professor, Education
Lander University
E-mail: caswell@lander.edu

Gordon W. Couturier
Professor, Information & Technology Management
University of Tampa
E-mail: gcouturier@ut.edu

Costas Efthimiou
Assistant Professor, Physics
University of Central Florida
E-mail: costas@physics.ucf.edu

Jason Farmer
Student, Information Science & Technology
Radford University
E-mail: jfarmer@radord.edu

Jean N. Gordon
Assistant Professor, Nursing
St. Thomas University
E-mail: pager@archwireless.net

Diane Grayson
Head, Centre for the Improvement of Mathematics,
Science and Technology Education
University of South Africa
E-mail: cimste@unisa.ac.za

Pedro F. Hernandez-Ramos
Assistant Professor, Education
Santa Clara University
E-mail: phernandezramos@scu.edu

Jessica Herron
Assistant Researcher, Computer Science
Clemson University
E-mail: jherron@clemson.edu

Mark Sudlow Hoyert
Associate Professor, Psychology
Indiana University Northwest
E-mail: mhoyert@iun.edu

Wendy L. Jordanov
Assistant Professor, Psychology
Tennessee State University
E-mail: wendy_jordanov@yahoo.com

Kathleen King
Associate Professor, English and Philosophy
Idaho State University
E-mail: kingkath@isu.edu

Ron Liss
Director, Distance Learning and Academic Innovation
Montgomery College
E-mail: ron.liss@montgomerycollege.edu

Ralph A. Llewellyn
Professor, Physics
University of Central Florida
E-mail: ralphl@pegasus.cc.ucf.edu

Derek Madden
Dean, Mathematics, Science & Engineering
Modesto College
maddend@yosemite.cc.ca.us

Coreen Mett
Professor Emerita, Mathematics
Radford University
E-mail: cmett@radford.edu

Richard Murphy
Adjunct Professor, Marketing
Nova Southeastern University
E-mail: dmurphy904@comcast.net

Susan S. Nash
Director, Online Curriculum Development
University of Oklahoma
E-mail: smithnash@ou.edu

Cynthia D. O'Dell
Associate Professor, Psychology;
Director, WOST
Indiana University Northwest
E-mail: codell@iun.edu

Roy P. Pargas
Associate Professor, Computer Science
Clemson University
E-mail: pargas@clemson.edu

John A. Rushing
Assistant Professor, Administration
Barry University
E-mail: jbarry@mail.barry.edu

Neil P. Sigmon
Visiting Assistant Professor, Mathematics
Radford University
E-mail: npsigmon@radford.edu

Malgorzata S. Zywno
Professor, Electronics and Computer Engineering
Ryerson University
E-mail: gosha@ee.ryerson.ca